SURREY

A COUNTY HISTORY

John Janaway

COUNTRYSIDE BOOKS

NEWBURY, BERKSHIRE

First published 1994
© John Janaway

COUNTRYSIDE BOOKS
3 Catherine Road
Newbury, Berkshire

ISBN 1 85306 309 6

The cover picture is by Andy Williams

The engraving on the title page of ruins at
Virginia Water has been taken from
Brayley's History of Surrey

Designed by Mon Mohan
Produced through MRM Associates Ltd., Reading
Printed by J.W. Arrowsmith Ltd., Bristol

Contents

Introduction

Surrey is something of an enigma. It is a county whose focal point lies beyond its boundaries and which has, therefore, been denied a major centre of its own. Its ancient borders appear to be the product of outside influences and pressures. On three sides of its rectangle of land they follow small streams and indistinct features known only to those who marked them out. To the north, the river Thames once formed a major boundary, but that natural barrier no longer delineates the county's edge, except for the mile or two between West Molesey and the Dittons. The land of Surrey looks rather like a leftover after everyone else has had their share.

On the geological map the county is like a section through a many layered cake or a piece of streaky bacon cut abruptly at either end. North Surrey is mainly a land of clay and barren sands. The dominant chalk ridge of the North Downs runs across the county from the thin line of the Hog's Back in the west to Tatsfield in the east. South and parallel to the Downs the greensand hills rise up and form, at Leith Hill, the highest point in south-eastern England. Beyond this ridge the oak bearing clays of the Weald pass into Sussex. With the exception of the Thames, the county's most important rivers, the Wey and Mole, have ignored these lines of alternating clay, chalk and sand, making their own contrary course right across them all.

Upon this land of natural contradictions man has planted his own pattern of settlement and communications. For more than 5,000 years he has been shaping the landscape that is Surrey today. The result is a county of remarkable contrasts, unique to those who make the effort to know it well.

Since the first century, when the Romans established London, the pattern of communications, and latterly of settlement too, has been dictated by the draw of the capital. London eventually outgrew the confines of its north Thames base and began to flood into Surrey. In successive waves, a tide of suburban building engulfed the northern part of the county, only to be stopped in this century at the very edge of the

4

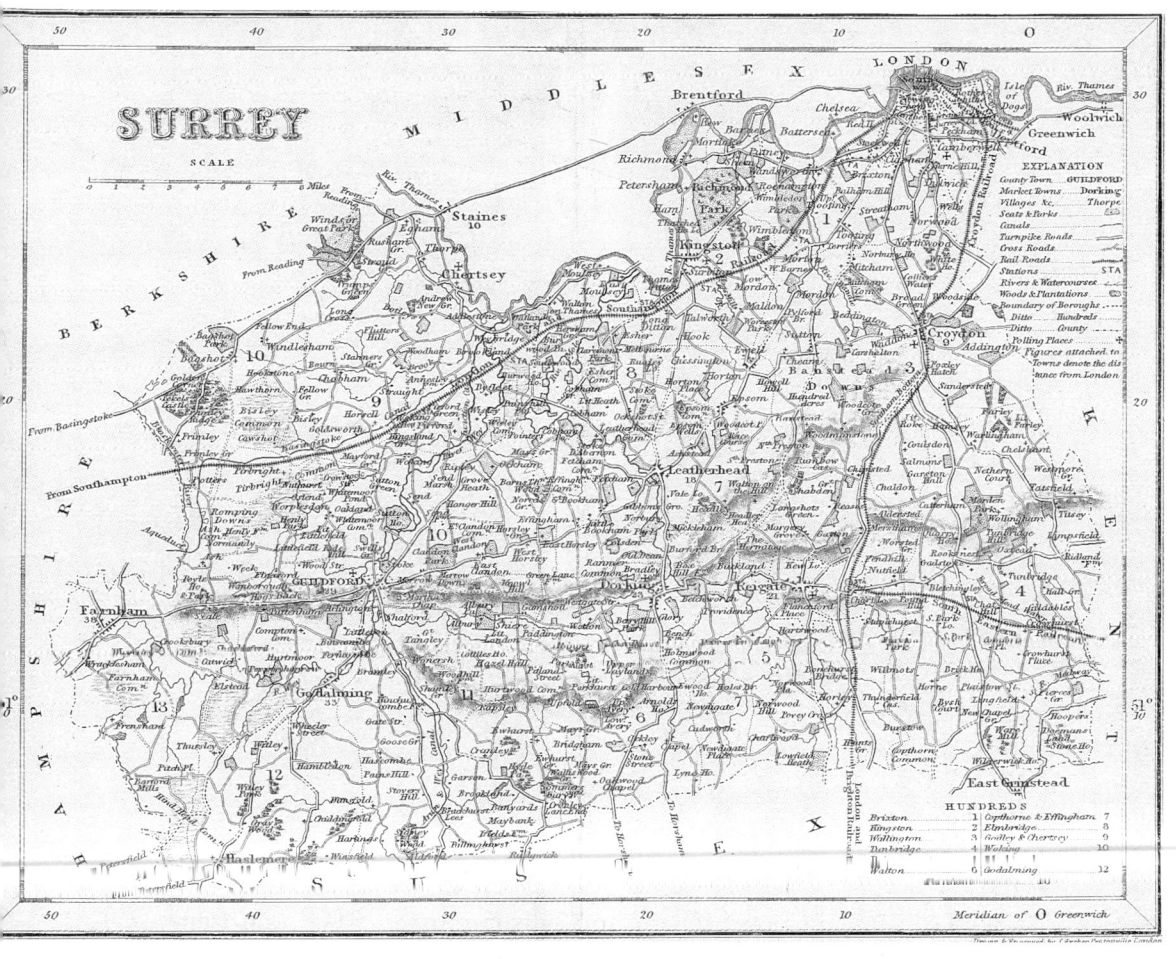

This map of Surrey by J. Archer can probably be dated to 1843 or 1844. It shows the railways which had been opened in the county up to May 1842 but not the first line to be completed after that date – the branch from Woking to Guildford, which opened in May 1845.

North Downs scarp. This spread of suburban London is reflected in the confusing boundary changes which the county has suffered during the last 100 years or so.

In 1889 the administration of the county was for the first time put on a corporate footing with the formation of Surrey County Council. The sacrifice for this new focus of identity was the loss of many suburbs adjacent to London. These included Southwark, Lambeth, Wandsworth, Bermondsey, Battersea and Camberwell. These places are firmly part of London as we know it and will not be included in this book.

In 1965 came further boundary changes when the now defunct Greater London Council came into being. Places which quite rightly

5

still identify firmly with Surrey were now absorbed into the capital's administration. These included Kingston, where Surrey County Council still has its headquarters, Surbiton, Richmond, Malden, Merton, Morden, Wimbledon, Mitcham, Sutton, Carshalton, Wallington, Coulsdon and Purley. Gone also was Croydon, which had been an independent county borough since 1889. The changes in 1965 also killed off the county of Middlesex but Staines, Sunbury, Ashford and adjacent villages were added to Surrey, thus destroying that natural boundary of the Thames. For the purposes of this book all these places are considered as part of 'present' Surrey.

With so much material to draw on it is obvious that this book must, in the end, be a personal selection of the many fascinating events in Surrey's history. The hope has been to write an entertaining book, which will also help the reader to follow the main threads of this unique county's past.

In my attempts to achieve this aim I have been helped by so many Surrey people, whom I have had the great pleasure to meet during my 35 years of interest in the history and archaeology of my county. This has particularly been the case during the last 13 years when I have been fortunate enough to be able to combine my hobby with my work. Partisan I may be, but I firmly believe that Surrey has the most friendly, enthusiastic and knowledgeable local historians in Britain. I thank them all for allowing me to draw so heavily upon their knowledge. Some people I must mention by name, either for particular information, for putting up with the gestation of this book or simply for the inspiration they have given me. Therefore, special thanks are due to John Whitbourn, Duncan Mirylees, Jeff Harwood, Peter Phillips, Roy Drysdale, Michael Hutt, Jean Tooke, Iain Wakeford, Marion Shipley, Tom Maile, Pat Ashworth, Janet Nixon, Ruth Drysdale, Sylvia Walker, Anne Johns and Mavis Davies. Thanks must also go to the Surrey County Council Libraries and Leisure Department and to Surrey Archaeological Society. I must not forget the help and encouragement I have received over the years from Nicholas Battle, who collared me one day in the street and persuaded me to write my first book over ten years ago.

Lastly, but by no means least, my thanks go to my wife, Sue, for her support, encouragement, practical help and advice, without which this book would never have seen the light of day. To her, this book is dedicated.

1

PREHISTORY

In about 1887, Frank Lasham, a Guildford stationer, printer and amateur archaeologist, made the acquaintance of a roadmender working in the Worplesdon area. This man took an intelligent interest in 'stoanes' and his keen eye had spotted a shaped core of flint, which had been thrown out on the road among a load of gravel during repairs. The flint was identified as a Palaeolithic hand axe, of a type which represents the earliest evidence of human activity in the area we now call Surrey.

Lasham traced the source of this road ballast to pits at Farnham. By encouraging the gravel diggers with financial rewards for any flints showing the handiwork of early man, Lasham was able to amass a collection of over 300 of these worked flints. They were not the first to be found in the area but, by publishing notes of his discoveries, he brought the importance of the gravel deposits around Farnham to the attention of a number of other researchers.

The Palaeolithic or Old Stone Age in Surrey spanned, perhaps, nearly half a million years. Throughout this time our area was a small part of a peninsula of land joined to the mainland of Europe. For long periods the climate was bitterly cold and vast sheets of ice covered the land to the north of Surrey. These cold periods lasted many thousands of years but were interrupted by warmer interludes, when average temperatures rose sometimes even above those of today. Elephants roamed the land while hippopotamuses splashed in river pools.

The river system of Surrey as it is today evolved during this period. As the rivers adjusted to oscillations in climate, they eroded their valleys, captured adjacent streams and changed course, leaving behind sheets of alluvial deposits mainly in the form of flint gravel. At Farnham these gravels lie on terraces above the present course of the river Wey, which at one time flowed through the valley now occupied by the river Blackwater. Each terrace has produced the characteristic hand axes of Palaeolithic man.

Palaeolithic man was a nomadic hunter and he is traditionally associated with animals of the tundra, particularly the mammoth. When conditions allowed, he followed his quarry north and in the summer months may even have hunted along the very edge of the ice sheets. His wanderings periodically brought him to the land we now call Surrey. His was a basic culture, an integral but small part of the ecology, which lasted for a vast period when set against the time of modern man. Only his flint tools have survived, discarded on a now extinct land surface, many of them battered and rolled by the river action which constantly resorted and redeposited the valley gravels.

Well over 1,000 hand axes have been recorded in the county, and while the gravels of Farnham are perhaps the best known source, there are a number of others. Many hand axes have been discovered in gravels associated with the river Thames, but it is sites at Walton-on-the-Hill on the North Downs and in the Limpsfield area in the east of the county which are of particular interest. Here worked flints are not associated with gravel as at Farnham but with clay-with-flints and brickearth deposits. Although periglacial conditions and erosion have changed the land surface in these places, the worked flints found may be close to where they were originally discarded. There have also been many isolated finds throughout the county and most Surrey museums have collections of them.

It is only towards the end of the Palaeolithic period that cultural changes are evident, marking the arrival of modern man about 40,000 years ago. Flint was still the main source material for his tools, from which he manufactured sharp blades and burins. This was a sophisticated hunting culture making use of other materials in addition to flint, such as antler and bone derived from the animals he hunted. However, evidence for early *Homo sapiens* in Surrey is very scanty and confined to just a few examples of his flint tools. These include a tanged spearhead found at Peper Harow, near Godalming, in the late 1920s and a large backed blade discovered at Leatherhead in 1983. Upper Palaeolithic man still hunted across an open tundra, his main quarry included reindeer, bison and horse.

Around 10,000 BC the climate began to show a marked improvement and gradually the treeless open tundra gave way to forests of birch and pine and later of oak, elm, lime and alder. These changes in habitat led to changes in man's hunting techniques, which ushered in the period known as the Mesolithic or Middle Stone Age. Flint was still the principal source for tools but the range of these tools showed that man had adapted very efficiently to the role of nomadic forest hunter/gatherer.

The most characteristic tools of the Mesolithic period are the microlith, tiny worked blades and points which were used in a variety of ways such

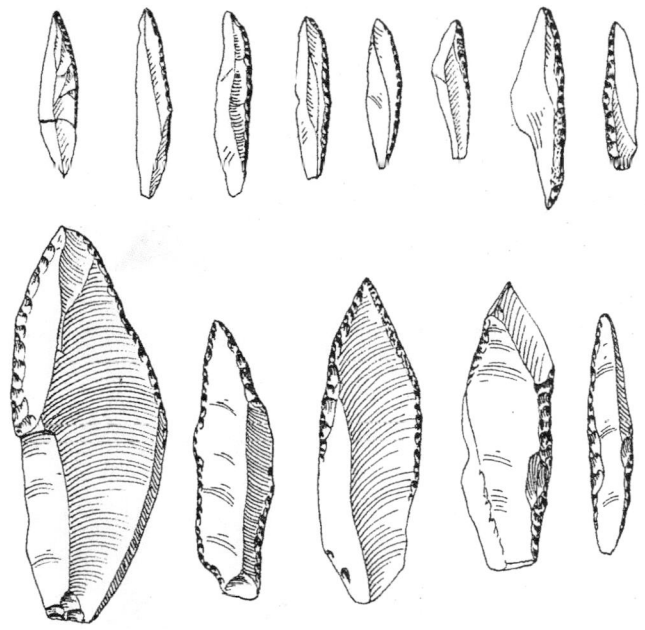

Examples of Mesolithic microliths found in Surrey. (Surrey Archaeological Society)

as the barbs of wooden harpoons, and the 'tranchet' axe, a very effective
tool for chopping wood. Many thousands of Mesolithic flint tools have
been recovered from all over Surrey. Indeed, in some areas in the
south west of the county, on the lighter soils of the Lower Greensand,
hardly a ploughed field or sandy heath is missing a few examples. Whilst
there is evidence that these areas were favoured during the Mesolithic
age, the distribution map of finds is undoubtedly distorted by the ease
of discovery in the open countryside of that part of the county. For more
than a century archaeologists have concentrated their field walking here
and ignored more difficult areas, especially where suburban housing has
now filled the fertile fields of a once entirely rural county.

There have been several claims for the discovery of the remains of
Mesolithic dwellings in Surrey. If true, they would represent the earliest
dwellings of any kind in the county. Pits excavated at Abinger in 1951
and at Weston Wood in the 1960s were thought to be the bases of
dwellings, which would have been roofed over with branches and
vegetation or perhaps even skins on a frame of wood. Currently,
archaeologists are dubious of these claims – the purpose of the pits
is not known and they may not even be of a Mesolithic date. Small
pits dug into gravel near Farnham, which were excavated just before
World War II, have also been claimed as 'pit dwellings' but, whilst these

9

pits might indeed have been of the right date, it is now suggested that they may be evidence of flint quarrying.

Around 6,000 BC, rising sea levels coupled with the sinking of the land on the east side of Britain, a process which continues to this day, led to the breaching of the land bridge with mainland Europe. Isolated from their cousins across the Channel, the Mesolithic groups in Britain developed their own variations of the basic types of flint tools, especially the microliths.

Armed with the highly efficient flint 'tranchet' axes, there can be little doubt that Mesolithic man was capable of clearing quite large areas of forest. Perhaps the Surrey landscape of this period consisted of fairly dense woodland interspersed with scattered man-made clearings of various sizes. Here single family groups or larger clans would camp for varying periods of time before moving on to follow the game or harvest fruits, berries and seeds. It is possible that some of the Mesolithic peoples independently developed the cultivation of certain useful plants in these forest clearings. There may even have been the semi-domestication of other animals besides the dog.

It has long been accepted that the present sterile acid heathlands of south-west Surrey are a man-made feature – the result of the over exploitation of a thin soil by early farming communities following the removal of the tree cover by axe and fire. There is evidence of a marked increase in population during the late Mesolithic period and perhaps the development of these heathlands began at this time as clearings were made to encourage grazing animals. Trade across the Channel, if not the actual invasion of peoples in large numbers, would also have spread the concept of animal husbandry and crop growing.

Whether through colonisation from mainland Europe, or via indigenous developments, or both, farming became established in southern England soon after 4,000 BC. These first farmers still used flint for many of their tools, for metallurgy was unknown to them. This period, known as the Neolithic or New Stone Age, also heralded a succession of technological developments, in particular the making of pottery. In Surrey, as in other parts of Britain, it is the Neolithic peoples who were the first to build structures whose remains in many cases are still visible today.

The most important of Neolithic structures in Surrey are a causewayed enclosure excavated recently at Yeoveney Lodge near Staines, a long barrow or burial mound discovered in the late 1930s at Badshot Lea, near Farnham, and the Stanwell cursus. This ritual processional way is at least two and a half miles long and consists of two parallel ditches dug about seven yards apart running north-north-west from Stanwell

The Mesolithic pit 'dwelling' at Abinger. (Surrey Archaeological Society)

village to disappear beneath the runways of Heathrow Airport. It was originally discovered by aerial photography but mistakenly interpreted as a Roman road. However, archaeologists have recently discovered late Neolithic pottery in the fill of the ditches and shown that this important structure, second only in size to the famous cursus in Dorset, pre-dates an adjacent Bronze Age barrow. The whole of this area of Surrey, part of Middlesex until 1965, has been shown by aerial photography and excavation to be rich in prehistoric features and must have been of particular importance to the peoples of that period, perhaps for ritual and religious reasons. Such structures also indicate the establishment of a complex society in Neolithic times.

Neolithic society must also have developed a sophisticated system of trade. Outside Surrey there is much evidence for the commercial mining of the best quality flint for trading over large areas. The nearest extensive flint mines so far discovered were on the South Downs in Sussex. Within Surrey such evidence is thin, although over the years there have been a number of claims for the discovery of flint mines. Of these, the most likely was discovered at East Horsley and investigated by archaeologists in 1949. Two medieval mine-shafts were found to have been dug into an area showing Neolithic mining activity, perhaps opencast.

Many Neolithic flint axes were ground and finely polished, an immensely time-consuming task, and were almost certainly objects of status or even ritual significance to their owners. Polishing techniques were also used on other stone objects such as flint scrapers and also on axes made of stone other than flint. Such axes are of great interest as evidence of trade, particularly during the late Neolithic period. Both chance finds and systematic excavation have, over the years, led to the discovery of more than a hundred axes fashioned from stone derived from places many miles beyond the bounds of the present county. The source of the material includes places as far apart as Cornwall, the Lake District, Wales, Northumberland and County Antrim in Northern Ireland.

Neolithic pottery was hand made, the earliest being thick-walled and lacking decoration. Later more finely potted types were developed with incised decoration of diagonal or transverse lines or chevron patterns. Neolithic man also used other materials such as bone and wood in the manufacture of artefacts but such finds are sparse in Surrey and consist mainly of antler picks and simple bone points.

The Bronze Age heralds, of course, the introduction of metallurgy to the British Isles. Raw copper was first worked here in about 2,500 BC, but its introduction was quickly followed by the discovery that an alloy of copper and tin, namely bronze, produced a hard metal ideally

12

suited for the manufacture of an extensive range of artefacts. These included daggers, spears, swords and particularly axes. Such axes became increasingly sophisticated in design as the Bronze Age progressed and had a development spanning over 1,000 years. There have been isolated finds of bronze axes over much of the county, whilst small hoards have been discovered in various places in south-west Surrey. In addition, large hoards of bronze artefacts including axes have been found along the Thames valley, most recently during archaeological investigation of a site at Egham. In common with a number of other hoards this major find, which included broken pieces of swords and ingots of bronze, was probably the scrap metal cache of a bronzesmith.

Finely crafted bronze swords began to make their appearance around 1,200 BC and several have been retrieved from the river Thames. However, despite the quality of such objects, Bronze Age man had not discarded flint as a medium in which to manufacture a large range of tools. This period represents the peak of flint craftsmanship and many exquisitely worked tanged and barbed arrowheads of the period have been found in Surrey. Bronze Age man also worked in antler, bone and wood.

The most visible surviving evidence of Bronze Age man is that of his round burial mounds or barrows, constructed in a variety of types. There were simple bowl barrows, bell barrows with a flat berm round the base of the mound, and the appropriately named saucer barrows with only a low mound in the centre surrounded by a ditch and bank. Whilst Surrey cannot boast examples as fine or numerous as those to be found in Hampshire and Dorset, there are still some significant examples. For example, there is a triple bell barrow on Crooksbury Common near Tilford and a ditched bowl barrow less than a mile away at Culverswell Hill. On Chobham Common there is a group of ten and on adjacent West End Common a line of four joined barrows. Barrows of this period usually covered pottery funerary urns containing cremations.

A major Bronze Age site, excavated in advance of the building of the M25 bridge over the Thames at Runnymede, produced extensive evidence of occupation on what had once been an island in the river. Here were found metalwork, evidence for the manufacture of horse trappings from antler and a wide range of domestic and personal items. These included loom weights and spindle whorls, indicating textile weaving, and imported goods such as bronze razors and pins, shale and bronze bracelets and amber beads – objects which related to the everyday lives of those who had made the island their home nearly 3,000 years ago.

The manufacture of iron objects in Britain is currently considered by

Bronze Age tanged and barbed arrowheads finely worked in flint. (Surrey Archaeological Society)

archaeologists to have commenced about 700 BC. Typically, the Iron Age period is most visually represented by its massively constructed hillforts, but archaeologists are now inclined to think that some of these forts had their origins in the Bronze Age. 'Iron Age' forts in Surrey considered to fall into this category are St Ann's Hill near Chertsey, St George's Hill, Weybridge, and Caesar's Camp near Farnham. These forts are orientated towards the north and the river system of the Thames and its tributaries. They reflect an emphasis on the rivers as the main thread of communication throughout the period preceding the Iron Age. There have been a variety of suggested functions for these forts. They were almost certainly tribal centres but, perhaps, also religious centres, and all important market places, particularly for the agricultural produce of expanding farming communities. The later Surrey hillforts – Hascombe, Holmbury, Anstiebury and Dry Hill, near Lingfield, were not constructed until 200 BC at the earliest and additionally served as strongly defended refuges during times of danger.

The vast majority of the Iron Age peoples in Surrey were farmers, living in round houses constructed on a framework of wooden posts. They husbanded animals including cattle, sheep, goats and pigs and kept horses and dogs. They grew barley, oats and emmer wheat. Evidence for their way of life in Surrey has been recovered by archaeologists from excavation of the remains of their farmstead settlements at a number of sites, including Hawk's Hill near Fetcham and Brooklands near Weybridge. The outlines of the field systems they constructed have survived in many places along the North Downs.

The Iron Age peoples were also sophisticated traders, who were responsible for the introduction of the first system of coinage into Britain. Large numbers of their coins have recently been discovered at the Romano-Celtic temple site at Wanborough, just north of the Hog's Back.

The role of the hillforts seems to have ceased abruptly about the time of Julius Caesar's incursions into southern Britain in 55–54 BC. The reasons for this are unclear but the 90 years before the final assimilation of Britain into the Roman Empire appear to have been a period of much change and regrouping. There is evidence for the expansion of peoples from the already heavily farmed chalk of the North Downs onto the light but still fairly rich soils to the south of the Hog's Back around Puttenham, Compton and Godalming. Tribal kingdoms were established, centred around proto-urban settlements, called oppida, although one has not been identified for the central southern territory, which would have included the Surrey area. It may have become part of the territory of the Atrebates, which included Sussex, and parts of Hampshire and Berkshire.

The pattern of settlement in prehistoric Surrey was controlled by several factors – the nature of the underlying rocks, giving a great variation in soil types and vegetation, the pattern of rivers and water supply and man's ability to control the environment. As his technology improved so did his influence upon the landscape. By the end of the prehistoric period, marked abruptly by the Roman invasion of AD 43, that influence was already well advanced in shaping the man-made landscape of Surrey which we see today.

2

THE ROMANS

When Julius Caesar landed on the south coast near Deal in 55 BC it is uncertain whether he came to conquer the Celtic tribes or simply to reconnoitre for the future. In the event, a number of circumstances, including gale damage to his fleet, meant that his first foray was a short one. Not deterred, he returned the following year with a larger and better equipped army, intent upon conquest. Britain had become a safe haven for the warring Belgic tribes of Gaul and it had even supplied troops fighting against the Roman legions on the mainland. Caesar was anxious to remove this threat to the north-western flank of his Gaulish conquests.

He found the tribes of southern Britain at war with each other. The most powerful tribe was the Catuvellauni, recent arrivals from Gaul, who had quickly carved out a substantial territory for themselves in an area to the north of the Thames, in what is now mainly Hertfordshire. Caesar's arrival soon had the effect of rallying the tribes behind Cassivellaunus, the leader of the Catuvellauni, who fought an initially successful but doomed campaign to destroy the Roman legions.

The route that Caesar took in order to seek out and destroy the centre of Cassivellaunus's operations, a hillfort beside the present settlement of Wheathampstead, has always been a source of argument and conjecture. On the route from Kent his army would have marched through north-eastern Surrey, but whether he turned his troops south to attack the occupants of Anstiebury, Holmbury and Hascombe is a matter of conjecture. The evidence of archaeologists certainly points to these forts having been abandoned at this time. Caesar's route north was blocked by the river Thames, wider but shallower in those days, but where did he cross in order to reach the heartland of the enemy?

It was the 16th century antiquarian and historian, William Camden, who thought he had found the answer:

"Tis impossible I should be mistaken in the place because here the river is scarce six foot deep, and the place at this day, from those stakes, is call'd Coway-stakes; I am the first that I know of, who has mention'd and settl'd it in its proper place.'

Camden was referring to the bend in the river upstream of the present Walton Bridge towards Oatlands, where there were once supposed to be lines of stakes across the river marking a ford. His ideas were accepted without question for more than 300 years.

The poet John Milton, writing in the mid 17th century, applied his fertile imagination to Camden's certainty:

'Whereof advertised, Caesar marches onward to the frontiers of Cassibelan, which on this side were bounded by the Thames; not passable except in one place and that difficult, about Coway Stakes near Oatlands, as is conjectured. Hither coming he descries on the other side great forces of the enemy, placed in good array; the bank sett all with sharp stakes, others in the bottom covered with water . . .'

This certainty as to Caesar's crossing point continued until well into the last century – the site even being marked on early Ordnance Survey maps. The truth is that there is no solid evidence that this famous crossing of the Thames took place near Walton. All that can be said is that the Roman army crossed somewhere, and it could just as well have been here as anywhere else.

Once across the Thames, Caesar's legions quickly stormed the citadel of Cassivellaunus, who soon after made his peace with the Roman leader. However, despite Caesar's successes in battle, Britain was not at this time to be absorbed. Further trouble in Gaul forced Caesar to abandon his campaign and return across the Channel. He left a southern Britain firmly in Rome's sphere of influence but not yet entirely subdued.

During the next 90 years or so the Surrey area of Britain was the subject of a power struggle between the Celtic tribes. Eventually either the Trinovantes or the Catuvellauni drove out the Atrebates in the west whilst in the east it is unclear whose rule held sway.

Caesar's invasions of Britain had in the main failed not because of the fighting skills of the Britons nor because of his lack of success in finding a safe haven for his fleet. The failure was due to the lack of stability in Gaul. Once the tribes there had been subdued and the efficiency of Roman administration applied, it was inevitable that Rome would turn again to invasion of Britain.

When the invasion came in AD 43, under Emperor Claudius, the Roman legions led by Aulus Plautius did not face the same problems as Julius Caesar had. Their landing place was carefully chosen to avoid any danger to the fleet. The current theory is that the legions came ashore in Chichester Harbour. They then made their way north through Sussex and Surrey with the local inhabitants offering little resistance. The local tribes quickly submitted to Roman rule. Indeed, many of them may have welcomed the Romans as allies. The lack of any significant evidence for a military presence at this time or, unlike Maiden Castle in Dorset, of any defence of Surrey's hillforts, supports this view.

Once the invaders were established the Romanisation of southern Britain began. The founding of London took place within seven years of the invasion and soon the task of linking settlements with a network of roads began. This process was to establish the main pattern of communication which has controlled the development of the Surrey area ever since. The major roads passing through the area ran from London to Silchester, crossing the Thames at Staines, and from London to Chichester, which crossed the river at Southwark. Long after the Roman civilisation in Britain had collapsed a superstitious population gave the former the name 'The Devil's Highway', whilst the latter was called Stane Street. Another road from the capital crossed the east side of the county and headed towards a port at Lewes. A further road diverged from Stane Street at Alfoldean, just over the present border with Sussex, and headed north-west towards Farley Heath. It almost certainly continued on through the Wey gap at Guildford to link up with the London to Silchester road. There is much research still to be done concerning this road, for its course has been traced with certainty for only the first few miles from Alfoldean. There must also have been a number of minor roads linking known Roman settlement sites, whose routes still await discovery.

Roman roads were constructed to follow the shortest possible route, deviating only to avoid impossibly steep hills or marshy ground. In Surrey they were mainly constructed of flint with gravel surfacing and today the best preserved sections are on Stane Street. From the B2033 road to Headley the Roman road is still used as a bridleway as it heads towards Mickleham Downs. The original metalling has survived in many places, particularly where it has been protected by overhanging bushes. Further along the route to Chichester the A29 through Ockley runs on the original Roman raised causeway, or aggar, for over two miles.

The Romans divided up the administration of their conquest upon Celtic tribal lines. Although it is unclear how this system worked in the Surrey area, it is likely that it was split between the Regni in the south, whose capital was Chichester, the Atrebates in the west, based on Silchester, and the Cantiaci in the east, with Canterbury as their centre. Much of the administration was carried out by Celtic

A group of visitors view the excavations of the Roman villa at Ashtead in 1925.

leaders who readily adopted the Roman way of life. It is important to emphasize that many 'Romans' were not born and bred in Rome. For example, most of the men of the legions which had spearheaded the invasion of Britain came from Gaul and the Iberian Peninsula. Hence, archaeologists and historians refer to people of Britain during the Roman period as 'Romano-Britons' as most of the population still consisted of the native Celts. It is also important to realise that their administrative areas bore no relationship to the area of Surrey, which did not exist until Saxon times.

The Surrey area was, therefore, very much on the boundaries of these territories and, as a result, lacks any major Roman town. However, a number of fairly extensive settlements have been identified. These include Staines, known as 'Pontibus', meaning 'at the bridges', from the two bridges adjacent to the settlement. One carried the London to Silchester road over the Thames, and a second probably crossed the river Colne. Despite its strategic position Staines was only a small town, covering four or five hectares at most. It may have developed simply as a stopping place at the river crossings, although it is possible that a fort may have been built here soon after the invasion, around which a settlement developed.

At Ewell a straggling development grew up along Stane Street, adjacent to the natural springs. At Merton and at Dorking there may have been posting stations on the London to Chichester road. In the Dorking area scatters of Roman material have been found at three different sites – Burford Bridge, where Stane Street would have crossed the river Mole, in Dorking town centre itself and at Pixham, where the Pippbrook joins the river Mole. The evidence for Roman settlements at Croydon and Burpham, north of Guildford, is also based on a scatter of material, but enough to suggest that at these places there was substantially more than just a single habitation.

The majority of the population of Roman Britain lived and worked in the countryside. Until recently there has been very little opportunity for archaeologists to investigate sites which could illustrate how the native population lived, the nature of their homes or how they were affected by a new administration and, perhaps, new masters. Now farmsteads have been discovered at Thorpe Lea near Egham and a rural settlement at Lightwater. Gradually some evidence, mainly in the form of pottery and simple iron tools, is being obtained, particularly from the contents of rubbish pits. These finds suggest that their everyday lives were probably little altered from what was experienced before the invasion.

It was the more successful Romano-Britons who occupied the villas. These buildings represented the controlling centre of working estates. Nearly 20 villa sites have so far been discovered in Surrey and they are fairly evenly distributed throughout the county, apart from an absence on the sandy heathlands of the north-west. The villa owners, whether incomers or Romano-Britons, wholeheartedly embraced the new culture and the Roman way of life. They warmed their homes with underfloor heating or hypocausts, such as the example found at Ashtead. They built elaborate baths like that discovered at Chatley Heath, near Cobham, and they also paved the rooms of their villas with mosaics – the best Surrey example coming from the villa on Walton Heath.

Practically all of Surrey's villas were in existence by the middle of the 2nd century and they remained in use, sometimes with interruptions, until the 4th century, when most of them appear to have been abandoned for good. However, it has been suggested that some sites in south-west Surrey may have continued to be occupied well into the 5th century, long after the normally accepted end of the Roman period in Britain.

Surviving evidence supports the view that Surrey had only a few industries during the Roman period and most of the prosperity of its inhabitants was based on agriculture. At Ashtead there was a tileworks

Staines Bridge in 1796 engraved from a sketch by Turner. The Roman bridge here was the first upstream of London and carried the road from London to Silchester.

attached to a villa, which may have come into operation shortly after the conquest. Here a large variety of tiles were manufactured, not only for roofing, but also for the construction of hypocausts. Products from the tile kilns here may well have been distributed over much of south-eastern England. Tiles were also made at the villa at Rapsley near Ewhurst, Horton near Epsom and probably at a site near Reigate.

Alice Holt Forest, just across the border into Hampshire, was a major centre for the manufacture of pottery. The industry has also been found in the adjacent parts of Surrey, at Farnham and also near Tilford. Here utilitarian, fairly coarse grey pottery, sometimes decorated with white slip and incised decoration, was made. Pottery kilns have also been discovered at Farley Heath and near Wisley, and it is postulated that a pottery industry must have existed near Leatherhead. The kilns in the Farnham area started early in the period but were at their height of production in the 4th century.

The Romans appear to have tolerated the religious beliefs of the native population, who, in return, had no trouble in accommodating some of the Roman gods, such as Mars, Jupiter, Apollo and Minerva. The sites of three Romano-Celtic temples are known in Surrey – at Titsey, Farley Heath and Wanborough. At the last two important discoveries of objects and offerings, mainly in the form of coins, have been made. The temple at Wanborough on the northern side of the Hog's Back has only recently been excavated. Finds made by archaeologists included hundreds of Celtic and Roman gold and silver coins and chain head-dresses decorated

Roman remains at Virginia Water but in this case imported from Leptis Magna to grace an 18th century landscape.

with standing wheels. Unfortunately, nationally important artefacts and information were lost on this site because of the attentions of illegal metal detector users, who ransacked some areas of the site before the archaeologists arrived. The temples at Wanborough and Farley Heath may have survived as important religious places until well into the 5th century.

For 250 years after Aulus Plautius's invasion, the Roman province of Britannia prospered. Then, during the 4th century, the threats to the stability of the Roman Empire, both from within and without, began to mount. Internal strife and civil war, barbarian incursions across its long frontiers, all contributed to the increasing strain which brought the Empire to breaking point. It is significant that the majority of Surrey's villas seem to have been abandoned by the end of the 4th century. Town settlements such as Staines experienced a revival during the 4th century following a period of stagnation, but they too had collapsed by AD 410. In that year the Emperor Honorius, with his western dominion on the verge of collapse, is said to have told the peoples of Britannia that they must, from now on, look to their own defence – in other words, Rome could no longer guarantee to supply troops to protect the province. They were needed elsewhere to defend the Empire in the west from barbarian raiders who were, at that very moment, at the gates of Rome.

3

ANGLO-SAXON SURREY

'In this year the Goths stormed Rome and the Romans never afterwards reigned in Britain.' These few terse words written by a 9th century scribe in the *Anglo-Saxon Chronicle* recorded the folk memory of events in AD 410, which began the final demise of the Roman way of life in Britain.

In fact, the decline of Roman Britain was not as instant as the chroniclers would have us believe. Its origins lay well back in the 4th century. Throughout the second half of that century the Roman Empire became increasingly threatened along most of its frontiers. To protect these borders, troops were progressively withdrawn from Britain. The army was the dynamo of the money-based economy and, without it, the Roman system began an inevitable collapse. There may also have been a decline in population at this time caused, perhaps, by epidemics of an unknown killer disease, possibly some form of plague. The economic breakdown was a major factor in the shift of people from the towns to the countryside. Surrey lacked any substantial Roman town but this decline can be seen in London, Silchester and Chichester and must, therefore, have had an effect on the area. Thus the seeds of major change had been sown long before the first Saxons arrived to settle permanently.

However, by AD 410, whilst the Goths attacked Rome, its outlying province, Britannia, was also under serious threat from barbarian tribes on the fringes of the Empire – the Irish to the west, the Picts to the north and various Germanic tribes who came to plunder from across the North Sea. In the 4th century, the building of a number of forts along the south coast, known as Saxon shore forts, had contained these plundering pagan hordes. Now, denied support from Rome, the Britons sought protection, particularly against the Picts, by enlisting the help of Saxon mercenaries. These Saxons from the north-west coast of Germany and Frisia were attracted by offers of money or land in return for their contribution to the defence of Britannia.

Surrey archaeologist, Rob Poulton, wrote of Surrey in 1987 that 'any aspect of the Saxon county is bedevilled by uncertainty and, in some cases, . . . a complete lack of useful archaeological evidence.' In attempting to reconstruct the possible, let alone the probable, story of Saxon Surrey, the historian must juggle scant and often doubtful documentary material with a meagre body of archaeological evidence.

The first Saxon mercenaries probably arrived in southern Britain in about AD 420, a decade or so after the final withdrawal of the Roman legions and the announcement of Emperor Honorius that the Britons must look to their own defence. Honorius's declaration has traditionally been used by historians and archaeologists to mark the end of Roman Britain. However, recent research has suggested that this apparent final rejection was not intended for Britain at all and that past scholars have simply mis-translated a name which actually referred to somewhere else in the Empire! Whatever the truth of the matter, we can be reasonably certain that the first Saxons arrived in Kent not long after and made their way inland along the river Thames.

In Surrey the evidence for these 5th century pagan settlers is confined to a scatter of burial sites to the north of the Downs, where many of them were stationed to guard the approaches to London. However, it is equally possible that these burials are the graves of the Saxon vanguard who died protecting the migration routes of their own kind along the Thames valley. Saxon cemeteries of the period have been discovered at Mitcham, Croydon and on the east end of the Hog's Back at Guildown, overlooking the site of Guildford and an important river crossing.

For about 20 years after the arrival of the first Saxon mercenaries all went well, but then events turned for the worse as far as the Britons were concerned. Instead of fighting the Picts, the Saxon troops turned upon their masters and were soon in control of substantial tracts of land in south-eastern Britain, including, perhaps, all of the Surrey area north of the Downs. According to the *Anglo-Saxon Chronicle*, the Britons sent a delegation to Rome in AD 443 to beg for help, 'but got none, for the Romans were engaged in a campaign against Attila, king of the Huns.'

Around AD 500 the Britons, led by a man of Roman descent, Ambrosius Aurelianus, had a great victory at the battle of Mons Bardonicus. The exact site of this battle is unknown today but may have been somewhere in Wiltshire or Dorset. For the next 50 years the Saxons seem to have been confined to the east side of the country. In Surrey there is some evidence that, whilst the Saxons occupied the north and east of the area, the Britons remained in control of south-west Surrey by agreement with the newcomers. It is notable that in that part of the county finds from the early Saxon period are almost entirely absent. This arrangement may have continued until well into the 7th century.

But what exactly did happen to the Romano-Britons in Surrey? Were

Abbey Mill at Chertsey – the first mill here was built by the monks of the abbey during the Saxon period.

they eventually forced from their lands and driven ever westward as more and more Saxon settlers arrived? Did they co-exist with their new neighbours, intermarrying and thereby over two centuries or more become absorbed? Finds of complete Roman pots from some early pagan Saxon graves at Croydon may suggest continuity. The Romano-Britons in Surrey were reputedly Christian but how much they held to the faith at this time is not known. They certainly seem to have had no influence on the early Saxon settlers in religious matters.

Experts consider that some place names, especially in south-west Surrey, might suggest the survival of Britons well beyond the 5th century. These include St Martha's Hill near Albury, which may be derived from the Latin 'martyrium', meaning a place of religious significance. Also, the pattern of archaeological finds from the pagan Saxon period from the 5th to the 7th century is suggestive of an agreement between the Romano-Britons and the Saxon settlers.

Roman farming estates in Surrey, centred around the villa, produced food mainly for sale in the market place, whilst the Saxon settlers grew crops principally for themselves. They were self-sufficient in the matter of feeding and clothing themselves. Faced with the collapse of the money economy the Britons of the Surrey countryside may well have adopted the Saxon way of life and thus have become integrated with them. Thereafter any archaeological record of their existence might prove to be indistinguishable from that of the Anglo-Saxons, who have traditionally been considered to be their replacements.

Whatever the real truth of the first 130 years of Anglo-Saxon settlement in Surrey, it is clear that after about AD 550 any land agreements between Saxon and Briton seem to have broken down. According to the *Anglo-Saxon Chronicle* there now followed 100 years or more of intermittent warfare before the Saxons emerged as sole rulers of most of the land which eventually became the kingdom of England. This was a period of minor kingdoms and sub-kingdoms, when the Saxons and perhaps those of Romano-British origin who had integrated with them, turned to fight each other for the supremacy of this green and fertile land. It was during these unstable times that Surrey probably first emerged as a sub-kingdom, although the names of any of its rulers have not survived.

The *Anglo-Saxon Chronicle* recorded that an important battle between rival factions took place in AD 568: 'In this year Ceawlin and Cutha fought against Ethelbert, and drove him in flight into Kent, and killed two ealdormen, Oslaf and Cnebba, at Wibbandun.' The site of the battle of Wibbandun is thought to have been in Surrey, traditionally either at Wimbledon, or Worplesdon, to the north of Guildford, or possibly near Chobham. It was, perhaps, at this time that the eastern limits of Surrey were established. The boundary is still marked by a substantial bank 3 metres high and 16 metres across on the border of Surrey and Kent near Westerham, but it is not known if the victors at Wibbandun were responsible for its construction. Surrey was a land to be fought over and at various times during the succeeding century it appears to have been a province of Kent, Wessex or the midland kingdom of Mercia.

In 596, according to the *Anglo-Saxon Chronicle*, Pope Gregory sent a group of monks led by Augustine to Britain to convert the pagan Saxons to Christianity. Augustine and his missionaries landed on the Isle of Thanet in Kent and by degrees, with many reverses, the conversion was successfully achieved. Christianity had reached Surrey by 666 when an abbey was founded at Chertsey by Abbot Erkenwald, who later became the Bishop of London and was instrumental in the building of the first cathedral of St Paul. The earliest surviving documentary record of Surrey's existence dates from 673 when Frithuwald, ruler of 'Sudergeona', gave a great estate for the endowment of the abbey. Frithuwald had to seek the permission of Wulfhere, ruler of Mercia – a clear indication of Surrey's status as a sub-kingdom at this time.

The name 'Sudergeona' means 'southern region', implying that Surrey must at one time have formed part of a much larger kingdom including, perhaps, Middlesex across the Thames. However, no documentary evidence survives to shed light on this suggestion and the larger unit had certainly ceased to exist by the early part of the 6th century. Surrey's

Excavations at Chertsey Abbey in 1861. (Surrey Archaeological Society)

eastern boundary may once have followed the line of the rivers Medway and Darent, now in Kent. It had become established along its existing line by the end of the 6th century, possibly, as mentioned earlier, following the battle of Wibbandun. Its western boundary is thought to have taken in parts of what later became Berkshire, but had settled to its present line along much of the border by the end of 7th century. The river Thames formed a natural northern limit whilst the southern boundary may have been the last to have been properly defined. The land along the border between Surrey and Sussex may have been a mixture of open pasture, suitable for summer grazing, and rich woodland.

At some time during the 7th century London was re-established as a major port. As the centuries passed the city was to increasingly influence the development of its southern hinterland, Surrey.

A Saxon cemetery of the 7th century has recently been excavated at Leatherhead. Here were found a number of pagan burials with a sparse but fascinating series of grave goods. These included socketed iron spearheads and iron knives, but of greatest interest was the discovery in one grave of a panther cowrie shell. A second grave, that of a child, contained the remains of a bead necklace – three of the beads being made from panther cowrie, two of amethyst and two of glass. The panther cowrie is found only in the Red Sea and these examples had

Medieval floor tile from Chertsey Abbey.

travelled a remarkable distance – a tribute, no doubt, to the importance these peoples placed on its properties as an amulet to ward off evil spirits. These were the graves of Anglo-Saxons who probably belonged to the transitional period between paganism and Christianity.

These people would have lived in timber-framed rectangular huts with thatched roofs. There were two types – one with an average floor area of about 60 square metres and the second version measuring only about 3.5 by 2.5 metres, but with the additional feature of a sunken floor cut a little under 1 metre into the ground. These smaller huts may have represented working huts, where occupations such as weaving took place, rather than living quarters. Finds of such buildings are scant in Surrey, though remnants have been discovered at several places including Farnham and Shepperton. These huts were loosely grouped in small hamlets, each forming a single farming community, self-sufficient in all but a few items. The hut dwellers wove their own cloth and probably made their own rough, grass-tempered pottery as well. It was a way of life which survived little changed in rural Surrey until well beyond the Norman Conquest.

4

VIKINGS AND THE ENGLISH NATION

'In this year King Brihtric married Offa's daughter Eadburh. And in his days there came for the first time three ships of Northmen and then the reeve rode to them and wished to force them to the king's residence, for he did not know what they were; and they slew him. Those were the first ships of Danish men which came to the land of the English.' This first visit of Scandinavian marauders, known variously as Danes, Norsemen or Vikings, was recorded in the *Anglo-Saxon Chronicle* as having taken place in AD 789 or shortly after. It was the start of a reign of terror which, with the occasional interlude, was to threaten the peace and well-being of the Saxon nation for the following 200 years or more.

The process of consolidation of that nation took a major step forward in AD 823 when King Egbert of Wessex defeated the Mercians and the men of Kent. Now the whole of southern England, including Surrey, submitted to the rule of Wessex. The Saxons were much in need of a united front at this time as the Viking raids became more frequent. Firstly they came in small pirate groups; then they came as well organised raiding parties; finally came vast armies intent on conquest and settlement.

In AD 851 a huge army of Danes arrived in 350 ships and invaded and plundered southern England. They came by way of the Thames and, according to the *Chronicle*, 'stormed Canterbury and London and put to flight Brihtwulf, king of the Mercians, with his army, and went south across the Thames into Surrey.' King Aethelwulf and his son, Aethelbald, leading an army of West Saxons, 'fought against them at Aclea . . . and there inflicted the greatest slaughter on a heathen army that we ever heard of . . . and had the victory there.' Tradition says that Aclea was Ockley near Dorking and the night before this great battle the Danes camped in the Iron Age fort of Anstiebury nearby. The battle was undoubtedly the bloodiest ever to take place on Surrey soil. A 12th century chronicler, Henry of Huntingdon, who obviously drew on earlier sources now lost, wrote of the battle:

'The battle was fought between armies of the greatest size, and was greater and more obstinate than any that had been heard of in England. You might have seen there the warriors charging together as thick as ears of corn, and rivers of blood rolling away the heads and limbs of the slain. God gave the fortunes of the war to those who believed in him, and ineffable confusion to those who despised him.'

This was a crucial victory for the men of Wessex. Christianity in southern England was saved, the heathen banished, at least for a short time, and the power of Wessex was in the ascendancy. The story of the battle of Ockley has all the right ingredients for a classic tale of the triumph of good over evil. However, although most modern 'experts' are in agreement that this dreadful bloodbath took place somewhere in Surrey, the identification of Aclea with Ockley is out of favour with them at present.

This battle left the kingdom of Wessex as the main defender of an emergent English nation. There was still a great deal of defending to be done for events at Aclea had failed to stem the tide of Viking plunderers. The Danes made the Isle of Thanet in Kent their stronghold and in AD 853 they inflicted defeat upon a combined army from Kent and Surrey, which had attempted to eject them. In 865 a large army landed in East Anglia, which they then used as a base and from there they rampaged through much of southern England. In 871 a second army arrived to augment their compatriots. The Vikings then raped and pillaged their way through much of the Thames valley, including Surrey, causing terrible suffering to the inhabitants.

During the construction of a railway line at Croydon in 1862, a Viking coin hoard was discovered. It contained Anglo-Saxon silver pennies from Wessex, East Anglia and Mercia, also Frankish coins from mainland Europe and, most remarkable of all, coins which had been minted by the Khalif Haroun-al-Raschid of Baghdad between AD 789 and 809. These Arab coins, which have upon them sentences from the Koran, had undoubtedly found their way to Croydon via Viking trading routes through Russia and thence to Scandinavia. They were considerably older than the majority of the coins found, which dated the burial of the hoard to some time between 871 and 875.

It was in 871, during the same month which saw the arrival of the second Viking army, that Aethelred, King of Wessex, died. He was succeeded by a man who was destined to play a major role in the foundation of the English nation, King Alfred the Great. Alfred was a wise and educated man but he was also a skilled general and shrewd politician. He was to prove his greatness during his many engagements with the Danes over the next 28 years.

However, events at the beginning of his reign were anything but auspicious. They began with defeat for the Wessex men at Reading and Wilton and culminated, seven years later, in Alfred's retreat to the island refuge of Athelney in the marshlands of Somerset. Throughout this period, the Danish Viking armies marched back and forth across England, wreaking havoc wherever they went. On many occasions the Anglo-Saxons sought peace by buying off the invaders with gold and silver or 'Danegeld'. The people of Surrey suffered in such raids, especially during the periods when London was known to be in Danish occupation. Chertsey Abbey was sacked, its buildings destroyed, its lands laid waste and the abbot and 90 monks slaughtered.

The turning point for Alfred and Wessex came in the 880s, at a time when the Danes were in control of Mercia, Northumbria and East Anglia, where many of them had settled permanently. A series of successes, both on the battlefield and politically, extended Alfred's kingdom over a large area of southern England, including London. The area was still, however, subject to raids by Vikings in search of booty. It was during one such raid in AD 893 that a Danish army was defeated at Farnham by a force led by Alfred's eldest son, Edward.

A substantial body of Danes had landed at Appledore on the south Kent coast and marched north-west to enter Surrey somewhere to the south-east of Guildford. The Wessex forces successfully outmanoeuvred the enemy and intercepted them at Farnham. Here a fierce battle forced the Danes to retreat northwards across the Surrey heathlands to the Thames. Pursued by the Anglo-Saxons, the Danes crossed the river somewhere between Windsor and Chertsey. Such was their panic that they were forced to swim across, having failed to find a suitable ford.

The Danes finally found refuge on an island in the river Colne to the north of Staines, where they were besieged. Unfortunately, by all accounts, events were not brought to a totally successful conclusion by the Wessex men. After a short while they abandoned their siege and went home because they had run out of food! The Danes then escaped to the safety of their kinsmen in East Anglia. Although the enemy was not destroyed, this victory for the Anglo-Saxons meant that for the rest of Alfred's reign Wessex, including Surrey, was safe from the Viking terror.

In defence of his kingdom, Alfred began the construction of a series of forts, or 'burhs', where his people could find refuge within an enclosure protected by banks and ditches. The building of these defences continued after Alfred's death, into the reign of Edward, and a record of them has survived in a contemporary document called the *Burghal Hideage*. Some burhs encompassed permanent settlements or towns, others were probably constructed purely as forts. The *Burghal Hideage* includes details of a burh at Escingum, now Eashing near Godalming, where a natural defensive position was enclosed. The use of the fort here was perhaps short-lived and it may have been quickly replaced by a burh at Guildford, where a thriving commercial centre was beginning to develop.

Alfred's schemes for ridding his kingdom of the Viking hordes met with some success and, when he died in 899, he left a legacy of relative peace compared with the horrors that had gone before. In Surrey and adjacent areas this peace was to last nearly a century.

The 10th century was not only a period of consolidation but also of growth. It was the century which saw the emergence of the English nation. The money-based economy was firmly restored and the familiar pattern of towns and villages developed. It can be inferred that small nucleated settlements had been established, for example, at Croydon, Dorking, Godalming, Leatherhead and Farnham. Many places in Surrey have origins as manors well before the start of the 10th century. Banstead is mentioned in a grant in AD 680 and the first surviving reference to Farnham is only eight years later. Epsom is recorded in a grant of land to Chertsey Abbey in 727, whilst the royal manors of Godalming, Leatherhead and Guildford are listed in the will of King Alfred the Great, which was written in about 880.

The royal manor of Kingston is of great interest because no less than six Saxon kings were crowned there between AD 902 and 958. The large block of grey stone upon which kings such as Edward the Martyr are supposed to have sat during the ceremony is preserved outside the Guildhall. Kingston may have been a royal residence as early as the 7th century but during the 10th century it developed as an important centre for river trade at a ford on the Thames.

Guildford was important enough to have a mint where silver pennies of King Ethelred and, perhaps, also Edward the Martyr were struck. Although other evidence is lacking, the layout of its major streets is clearly the product of Saxon town planning.

It was during the 10th century that the administration of Surrey based on divisions known as hundreds was developed. In essence, much of this system was to survive for 1,000 years. Each hundred had its own regular moot or court presided over by the king's representative, the reeve, which considered criminal matters, for example, and also levied taxes.

Coronation Stone of the Saxon Kings
KINGSTON UPON THAMES

The stone at Kingston supposedly used as the throne at the coronations of six Saxon kings including Edward the Martyr.

Each hundred consisted of ten tithings, each tithing being represented by ten men who stood surety for each other. The moot would gather at the most central or convenient place in the hundred and not necessarily at the most important centre of population. Thus, although Godalming was the meeting place of a hundred, Guildford was not, being within the hundred of Woking. In east Surrey, Cherchefelle Hundred was named from its chief settlement, which later became known as Reigate. Almost the exact centre of the county's most easterly hundred was Tandridge and this small settlement provided both the meeting place and the name of the hundred.

This period also saw the development of the shire and the setting up of shire courts. These met twice a year and were presided over by the king's direct representative, the shire reeve, a name which soon became corrupted to sheriff. It was the sheriff's responsibility to administer royal property in the shire, to collect rents from the royal lands and profits from the court fines. Surrey's first sheriff was appointed 1,000 years ago, although his name has not survived. The post still exists to this day and each year a new High Sheriff of Surrey is appointed by the Queen. The Sheriff still has a role to play in the administration of justice at the Crown Court and is also the official returning officer for elections to Parliament.

In AD 980 the Vikings returned with a vengeance and from that moment on their raids became ever more frequent. In 994 almost the whole of southern England, including Surrey, was ravaged and temporary peace bought with £16,000. The Vikings have left very little archaeological evidence for these raids in Surrey. However, in June 1981 a 10th century Viking sword was dredged up from a gravel pit near Chertsey. It may have come from a silted up meander of the river Thames, where it was possibly lost during a raid on Chertsey Abbey. The sword was in a remarkably good state of preservation, complete with iron pommel and guards still carrying traces of silver and copper inlays. This very rare find also carried the name 'Ulfberit' inlaid on the blade. Over 100 swords bearing this maker's name have been found in a wide area of Europe stretching from Ireland to Russia – a testament to the far-reaching influence of the Vikings as raiders, traders and, finally, settlers.

For England, the outcome of 30 years of almost continuous warfare was that a Viking king, the Dane, Cnut, ascended the throne of England in 1017. But Cnut proved to be a shrewd politician and a better ruler of England than many of his Saxon predecessors. To cement his right to the English throne he married Emma of Normandy, wife of his erstwhile enemy, the unfortunate King Ethelred the Unready, who had died in 1016. Emma returned from the safety of Normandy for the marriage, abandoning there her two sons by Ethelred, Alfred and Edward. Edward was later to become king of England, popularly known as Edward the Confessor, but poor Alfred came to an untimely end in a chain of macabre incidents which culminated in scenes of unimaginable horror at Guildford in 1036.

When Cnut died late in 1035 he was succeeded by his only son by Emma, Harthacnut. At the time, the new king was in Denmark and for various reasons was unable to cross to England to claim his throne. Meanwhile, many of the English leaders, headed by Earl Godwin, who had been one of Cnut's chief advisers, were championing the right of Harold, an illegitimate son of Cnut, to be king. Into this uncertain period of English history walked the apparently unsuspecting Alfred who, as a son of King Ethelred, was also a claimant to the throne.

The series of events in 1036 are confusing and reports often contradictory but from these it is possible, perhaps, to piece together some semblance of the truth.

Alfred landed from Normandy at Southampton, reportedly to visit his mother at Winchester, with an entourage of 600 followers. He was greeted by Earl Godwin in a friendly fashion and offered generous hospitality. However, by some trick or other he was persuaded not to go to Winchester and he and his party were conducted to Guildford by some of Godwin's men. Here, welcoming friends suddenly turned into vicious foes. Alfred and his men were seized and bound, then beaten and tortured. When as much pain as possible had been extracted from each victim, nine out of every ten were slaughtered. When 60 were left another nine out of ten were also condemned, leaving but six to survive this bloody episode.

Alfred himself was conveyed to Ely but, somewhere along the route or perhaps at Guildford, his eyes were pulled out. At Ely his torturers showed no mercy and his end, if we are to believe the Abbot of Jerveaux writing in the 12th century, was almost too horrendous to imagine:

'Indeed some say, that the beginning of his bowels being drawn out through an opening in his navel, and tied to a stake, he was driven in circles, with iron goads, till the latter parts of his entrails were extracted.'

There was rightful indignation at such barbarous cruelty even amongst supporters of Earl Godwin. The *Anglo Saxon Chronicle* scribes wrote that 'no more horrible deed was done in this land since the Danes came and peace was made. Now we must trust to the beloved God that they rejoice happily with Christ who were without guilt so miserably slain.' Godwin was, not surprisingly, out of favour until the death of Harthacnut in 1042, but he was too powerful a man for true justice to avenge the fate of poor Alfred. The 'miserably slain' appear to have been hastily buried on Guildown overlooking the town of their suffering. Here their mutilated remains were rediscovered in the 1920s, buried amongst the graves of the first Saxon settlers, whose deaths had preceded theirs by more than 500 years.

5

CONQUEST AND THE SURREY DOMESDAY

By one of those strange turns of history, it was the unfortunate Alfred's brother, Edward, who became king of England in 1042. Edward, a pious man who later earned the epithet 'the Confessor', had spent 25 years in exile across the Channel under the protection of the Duke of Normandy. His affinity with the Duke's people naturally led him to gather many Normans about him at court, one factor which brought resentment and finally open opposition amongst his English subjects. Earl Godwin, whom Edward understandably seems never to have trusted, was the most powerful of those Englishmen. Godwin died in 1053 but was succeeded by his son, Harold, who eventually became the centre of power in the land, even above the king. Edward the Confessor had promised his throne to the Duke of Normandy, but Harold was considered by many to be the obvious successor to a benign and Christian monarch who was later raised to the sainthood.

Edward's Christian principles gave the lead throughout his kingdom and brought a surge of church building in communities both large and small. The parish church of Stoke D'Abernon is claimed to have the earliest surviving work in a Surrey church – the remains of an apse and a doorway which are said to date from the 7th century. The church also, incidentally, has the oldest surviving church brass in England – that of Sir John d'Abernon dated to 1277. However, it is no coincidence that several Surrey churches incorporate in their fabric features which indubitably date from the reign of Edward. The tower of St Mary's in Guildford is built in flint and chalk, with typically Saxon small double-splayed windows and shallow pilaster strips. The tower would originally have been topped with a wooden belfry but this was later replaced by the crenellations seen today. Compton church also has a Saxon tower and a number of other features thought to date from the period.

St Peter and St Paul, the parish church of Godalming, has at its core a Saxon church, but nothing of it is visible from the outside. However, up in the bellringers' chamber there are two blocked double-splayed circular windows which would originally have been in the east wall of the Saxon nave. The Saxon chancel arch survived until 1879 when it was removed during Victorian 'restoration'. Victorian church builders were also responsible for the demolition of the church at Hascombe, which many consider to have been of an early date. Having survived almost intact for perhaps more than 900 years, this beautiful little church was razed to the ground in 1864. In mitigation, it has to be said that its replacement, designed by Henry Woodyer, is undoubtedly one of the best churches of its type and period in England.

Edward the Confessor died on 5th January 1066 and Harold was duly installed as the new king. Meanwhile, in Normandy, Duke William, who had been promised the English throne by Edward, began his plans to take it by force. Harold had but nine months to reign.

The story of the battle of Hastings and the Norman conquest of England must be well known to most readers and will not be repeated here. Suffice to say that, during his short reign, Harold, England's last Saxon king, showed himself to be a good leader of men. He undoubtedly had most of the nation behind him but his throne was threatened from two fronts. Firstly, by Harold Hardrada, King of Norway, whose claim to England descended via Harthacnut. Harold of Norway landed with a Scandinavian army in Yorkshire but was defeated and killed by Harold of England at the battle of Stamford Bridge on 25th September 1066. The English king had no time to recover from this bloody encounter before he heard of Duke William's landing at Pevensey. Within a mere 18 days Harold had tidied up matters in the north and marched south, gathering reinforcements as he went, to face a Norman army of hand-picked fighters. Amongst Harold's army there were undoubtedly men drawn from all levels of society in Surrey. From trained warriors to simple peasants, most were to meet the same fate as their leader on the autumn battlefield of Hastings.

After Hastings, William sought possession of the key to England, London. It proved impossible to storm the capital from the south across London Bridge. Therefore, the Norman army marched westwards across Surrey, leaving a trail of destruction in its wake. For many Surrey folk their first sight of a Norman soldier was probably their last. The army moved into Hampshire, then Berkshire and finally crossed the Thames at Wallingford, coming down on London from the north. William was in sight of the city when he received the submission of its leaders. On Christmas Day 1066, at Westminster Abbey, he was crowned king of England.

Despite continuing insurrections during the early part of his reign,

William soon consolidated his hold on his new possession. As the *Anglo-Saxon Chronicle* reported sombrely of William's enemies:

'Some of them were blinded
And some driven from the land.
So were the traitors to William
Brought low.'

During the next 20 years the English ruling classes were replaced by William's Norman followers and England became a nation ruled by a foreign elite. By right of conquest William personally took possession of all the land except that belonging to the church. He then rewarded his followers with gifts from his vast new gains in return for military service as required. William was shrewd enough, however, not to give any individual too large a holding in one place, in case they should use it as a power base from which to turn against him.

Part of William's strategy to subjugate the Saxon population was the construction of castles, which were designed as bases for the control of the surrounding countryside. The castle also provided a safe haven in times of threat and many eventually developed into massive structures capable of withstanding lengthy sieges. Some, like that at Guildford, were built under William's direction but others were the work of his barons. The royal castle at Guildford is Surrey's earliest example and was probably originally built about 1070. The chosen site guaranteed that every inhabitant of the Saxon borough would feel intimidated by the castle's looming presence. It also guarded an important river crossing and the entrance to a narrow gap in the North Downs.

To construct the castle, a projecting spur of chalk downland was cut through by the digging of a deep ditch. The resultant spoil was then heaped upon the spur itself to form a mound or motte. The flat top of the motte was then encircled with a wooden palisade to form a keep. A more extensive palisade, and probably also a ditch, enclosed the motte and a triangular area to the south-west known as the bailey. The bailey contained the buildings which housed the garrison, always at the ready to ride out in pursuit of the rebellious. Gradually over the years all the wooden structures were replaced in stone, much of it being a locally found type of hard chalk known as clunch. The present keep dates from the 12th century and is built mainly in Bargate stone, which was quarried in the Godalming area. It would still dominate the town but for the Sydenham Road multi-storey car park which stands almost immediately behind it! Guildford Castle played a significant part in the history of medieval Surrey and will be mentioned again later.

Reigate Castle as it appeared in the 18th century

Bletchingley Castle was built by Richard de Tonbridge, founder of the de Clare dynasty, soon after the Norman Conquest and consisted of a ringwork with an outer bailey. As at Guildford, any defensive palisades and buildings were originally in wood and later replaced in stone. The castle was demolished in 1264 during the battles between Simon de Montfort and Henry III. Reigate Castle is perhaps a little later than either Guildford or Bletchingley and was probably originally constructed in about 1090 with, as at Bletchingley, a ringwork and bailey rather than a raised motte. It was the Surrey base of the de Warrennes, sometime Earls of Surrey. Now only earthworks remain, decorated by a feeble gatehouse constructed in 1777 from original stone left lying about the site of the demolished castle.

At Abinger, near the church, stands a small motte which was excavated in 1950. Here archaeologists uncovered a series of postholes on the top of the mound, which showed that it had once been surmounted by a wooden watch tower on stilts surrounded by a stockade. A date in the late 11th or early 12th century, has been suggested for the construction

39

Hascombe church in 1800 from a painting by H. Petrie. This church was demolished in 1864.

of this small 'castle'. Similar mottes existed at Walton-on-the-Hill and possibly also at Chessington, Cranleigh, Godstone and Ockley.

The motte and keep which formed the basis of Farnham Castle were built in 1138 by Henry de Blois, Bishop of Winchester, and brother of King Stephen. Later in the same century the keep was rebuilt and much of it survives to this day, despite being blown up during the Civil War of the 17th century. Unusually, its base encloses the original motte and had only very rudimentary accommodation for use as a safe haven in dire emergencies, the main living quarters being arranged in a courtyard below it.

Whilst these castles successfully helped to control any threat from within William's new kingdom, the greatest potential dangers came from without. In 1085 the *Anglo-Saxon Chronicle* told that 'in this year people said and declared for a fact, that Cnut, king of Denmark, son of King Swein, was setting out in this direction and meant to conquer this country'. William was in Normandy at the time but returned quickly to face this possible challenge. He brought with him a large army which included many mercenaries from France and Brittany. They were billeted all over the country at his Norman followers' expense and 'they provisioned the army each in proportion to his land.'

A romantic 19th century image of a windmill. Windmills were not introduced into Britain until the 12th century.

In the event, the Danish invasion did not materialise and part of the army was dispersed. A core was, however, retained through the winter because William rightly felt that his possessions, both England and Normandy, remained under threat. The situation set William thinking and '. . . at Gloucester at midwinter . . . the King had deep speech with his counsellors . . . and sent men all over England to each shire . . . to find out . . . what or how much each landholder held . . . in land and livestock, and what it was worth.' Principally he wanted to know, perhaps, how much it was worth for tax purposes and what size of army it could support, bearing in mind that Danish ships might appear on the horizon at any moment. The written record of this survey, completed in less than a year, came to be known as the Domesday Book. It was proof of a highly organised and sophisticated nation.

The Anglo-Saxon chronicler had to reluctantly agree that a very thorough job was done: '. . . so very narrowly did he have it investigated

The tower of St Mary's church, Guildford, was built before the Norman conquest of England.

that there was no single hide or virgate of land nor indeed . . . one ox nor one cow nor one pig which was there left out, and not put down in his record; and all these records were brought to him afterwards.'

The Surrey survey covers an area identical to that of the county which survived until the creation of London County Council in 1889, when a number of parishes in the north-east were absorbed into the new administration. In all, 142 separate places are named and there are also a further 14 holdings listed anonymously. Two settlements in the ancient Surrey are listed as boroughs, Southwark and Guildford, but only the latter remains within the present county. Here Domesday lists 80 dwellings, 75 of which were owned directly by King William. From this we can deduce that Guildford was only a small town of perhaps no more than 700 people. However, the record is not as complete as the Anglo-Saxon chronicler would have us believe – Guildford had a castle by this time and at least one church, St Mary's, but neither are mentioned.

All the other places listed in the Surrey section are assessed as agricultural units. The record shows the extent of their arable land, assessed by how many plough teams it supported, and the acreage of meadows for grazing animals. The inhabitants are listed in four categories – villeins (villagers), bordars and cottars (in Surrey both smallholders) and serfs (slaves). Woods are shown according to how many pigs were paid as an annual rent for the right of pasturage on the acorns, roots and beechmast or 'pannage' of the woodland floor. Also recorded are the values of watermills and fisheries. Finally, most entries give three separate values for the holding – in the time of King Edward the Confessor, after the Conquest and at the time of Domesday. Thus, as an example, the entry for Ockham reads, in translation, from the Phillimore edition of the *Surrey Domesday Book* published in 1975:

'Richard holds Ockham himself, in lordship. Aelmer held it from King Edward. Then it answered for 9 hides, now for 1.5 hides. Land for 4 ploughs. In lordship 1 plough; 6 villagers and 2 smallholders with 2 ploughs. A church; 3 slaves. 2 fisheries at 10d; meadow, 2 acres; woodland, 60 pigs. The value is and always was 100s.'

The Lord of Ockham was Richard de Tonbridge, who was the founder of the de Clare family, who acquired the name from his major land holdings in Suffolk. In Surrey, Richard held no less than 38 manors which, in addition to Ockham, included Chelsham, Woldingham, Beddington, Mickleham, Walton-on-Thames, Betchworth and Bletchingley. It was Bletchingley Castle which became the main base for the family's activities in Surrey.

In the time of Edward the Confessor Ockham had been assessed at 9 hides. A hide was a unit of land for tax purposes, which varied in area according to factors such as the quality of the soil and its consequent agricultural yield. Therefore, the actual area could vary from 60 to 180 acres. By 1086, Ockham's assessment had dropped to 1.5 hides, despite the fact that its value had remained the same. Present day Domesday experts still argue the reasons for this and, as yet, no established explanation has been forthcoming.

Many Surrey manors do show a drop in value immediately following the Conquest – the possible explanation for this being that the loss was a direct result of the destruction caused by William's army as it rampaged across the county after the battle of Hastings. For example, Domesday says of Chipstead, another of Richard de Tonbridge's Surrey manors: 'Value before 1066 £7; later 100s; now £6.' Clearly, this manor had not fully recovered even 20 years later. Richard's manor of Shalford was worth £16 before the Conquest when it was held by 'two brothers' whose actual names were not recorded by the Domesday commissioners. Perhaps there were no original inhabitants left in the place to remember the names of the Saxon owners, for it had suffered greatly under the Norman invaders and its value post-Conquest had sunk to £9. However, by 1086 it had not only recovered but was now worth in excess of its pre-Conquest value at £20.

The Domesday entry for Ockham includes a church but for more than half the manors listed there is no such record. Both Guildford and Reigate (Cherchefelle) are known to have had churches by the time of the Norman Conquest although they are missing from Domesday. The reasons for these omissions are obscure. In contrast, some places are recorded as having more than one church – Epsom, Sutton and Godalming had two, whilst the now comparatively small village of Bramley had three. One of these was probably the church at Hascombe, a settlement which is entirely missing from Domesday.

The Ockham entry is also of particular interest because it records two fisheries. These would probably have consisted mainly of eel traps on the river Wey, the eel being a popular addition to the medieval diet. Just downstream from Ockham at Byfleet, eels are specifically mentioned as the product of its fisheries. All the Surrey fisheries were on the Thames or the Wey, with the exception of that at Limpsfield, which must have been on a small tributary of the river Eden. No fisheries existed on Surrey's other major river, the Mole, according to Domesday, but perhaps, like the missing churches, they were there anyway.

There is no mill listed at Ockham and the earliest surviving reference to a mill there dates from the 13th century, but just under half of Surrey's settlements had at least one mill. Dorking had three, worth an annual rent of 15s 4d. Some settlements shared mills, as is proved by entries such as that for the Bishop of Bayeux's holding in Fetcham. This included 'the sixth part of a mill and the third part of another mill'. All these mills were, of course, watermills for the grinding of corn – the windmill was not introduced into Britain until later in the medieval period. Therefore, it is curious that mills are also recorded for some settlements situated on the Downs, away from surface streams. For example, at Banstead there was a mill worth 20s – it must have been a detached property situated some distance from its manor on the upper reaches of the Hogsmill at Ewell or on the river Wandle at Carshalton.

Hascombe, mentioned above, is only one of many Surrey settlements which have no entry in Domesday. Most of these 'missing' places are situated in the extreme south of the county, where the Wealden clay made arable farming difficult if not impossible. Although still well

The windmills at Outwood in the 1900s. The post mill on the left was built in the 17th century and has been restored. It is now the oldest working windmill in Britain. The smock mill became derelict and was blown down some years ago.

forested in the 11th century, this area would also have had substantial areas of open pasture well suited to summer grazing. There is evidence to suggest that many small settlements did exist here at the time of Domesday. However, details of them may well have been included in the entries for manors further north to which they were attached.

The Domesday Book formed the basis for taxation for some considerable time after it was completed. Information on those liable to pay was of the utmost importance, so the final document was arranged not by place but by landholder. Thus in Surrey it begins with the properties of King William himself, followed by the Archbishop of Canterbury, the Bishop of Winchester and so on. It is the record of Norman lordship over a Saxon people. In Edward the Confessor's time most of Surrey was held by Saxons but by 1086 they had been almost entirely replaced by William's followers. Only a very few remained – like Wulfwin, who held Byfleet from his overlord, the Abbot of Chertsey, just as he had more than 20 years before. It is no coincidence that the most minor landholder in Surrey, listed at the very end of the document, was the Saxon, Wulfwy the Hunter, who held Littleton near Guildford worth a mere 20 shillings.

6

MAGNA CARTA AND BEYOND

The hundred years or so following Domesday were a period of great strife throughout much of England. Civil war between barons supporting rival claimants to the English throne was then followed by war between the barons and the monarch to decide who really controlled the country. In Surrey, these battles centred on the rivalry between the de Clare family whose base in the county was Bletchingley Castle and the de Warrennes who held the castle at Reigate.

The two families were firmly on opposing sides when the fight between King John and a large section of the English barons came to a head in 1215. Richard de Clare was one of the leaders of the barons, William de Warrenne, a staunch supporter of the King. It can safely be said that King John was not such a bad man as his enemies would have us believe. The final revolt against his rule had its origins amongst a number of lesser northern barons, who moved south gathering further malcontents as they went. Each claimed a catalogue of injustices inflicted upon them by the king. However, as the historian A.L. Poole wrote, 'The stories of personal wrongs, which they had suffered at the hands of the king, rest either on fabrications concocted many years later to blacken the character of John, or on evidence so confused as scarcely to deserve serious consideration.'

It is significant that, as the storm clouds gathered, John continued to have the support of most of the senior barons, those of experience and diplomacy, men who stood for the good of the whole country not just for their own selfish interests. John had no wish for further battles and sought conciliation. The one man whom both sides respected was Stephen Langton, Archbishop of Canterbury. It was undoubtedly he who was the guiding hand in all the negotiations, which led to the sealing of the Great Charter or Magna Carta at Runnymede in Surrey in June 1215.

Much of the myth which still survives today surrounding the events of 1215 is the product of the fertile imagination of Surrey author,

Martin Tupper, who in the mid-19th century wrote a best-selling historical novel entitled *Stephan Langton: or the days of King John*. In his book Tupper described John as a bad villain in the best traditions of Victorian melodrama. In one episode, John carries off the love of Stephen's life to Tangley Manor, near Wonersh, to have his wicked way. In another fictitious incident, Emma the woodman's daughter, 'a nut-brown maid with ruddy cheeks and coal-black eyes and hair', prefers to step back into the crystal waters of the pool in which she is bathing rather than submit to John's advances. She is drowned as a result. Even today the pool, near Albury, which Tupper chose for this dastardly deed is said to be haunted by poor Emma's presence and most local people know it as the Silent Pool.

Tupper has Stephen Langton being born at 'Friga Street' or Friday Street, where there is still a pub named after the Archbishop. In fact, nothing is known of Langton's origins and there is certainly no evidence to connect him with Surrey. The 'good' barons who sought to restrain the King's excesses were said by Tupper to have met in a cave beneath Reigate Castle. The cave, which still exists, actually started life as a sand mine but it is still known as the 'Barons' Cave' thanks to Tupper. Historian H.E. Malden rightly dismissed this claim when he wrote that 'Blechingley Castle would have been a happier suggestion, but the preliminary meetings of the baronial party had been at St Albans, Bury St Edmunds and London, and the actual march of their army was from Stamford to London. They only passed through the extreme northern edge of Surrey when they went up to Runnymede to meet John.'

King John was at Windsor and the barons crossed the Thames at Staines. Therefore, it was in a green Surrey meadow by the banks of the great river that John put his seal to a draft agreement. In the space of four days scribes turned this agreement into one of England's most significant documents. The charter's clauses included guarantees of certain feudal rights, confirmation of the free customs and liberties of London and other cities, towns and ports and the affirmation of the principles of justice. It was a major milestone upon the long constitutional road which finally led to democracy for all Englishmen.

It seems certain that John was sincere in his wish for a peaceful settlement with the barons when he placed his seal upon Magna Carta. The barons were not of the same mind and were soon plotting to bring over Louis, the Dauphin of France, to usurp the king. Louis landed in May 1216, the French fleet being under the command of 'Eustace the Monk', and by the 21st of the month Louis had joined the barons in London. The excuse for this invasion was that John had been tried by the court of France in 1203 for the murder of Arthur of Britanny and

47

had been condemned to forfeit his crown. This justification was a fake. John retreated quickly through Surrey to Winchester and all the castles of the county, including the royal castle at Guildford, fell to Louis. John was eventually driven further west to Corfe in the Isle of Purbeck, where he and his forces recuperated before launching a counter attack.

It was during his attempts to regain control that John was taken ill and he died on 18th October 1216 in the castle at Newark. According to A.L. Poole, 'he was buried, as he had desired, near the shrine of his favourite, his patron saint St Wulfstan, at Worcester where his memory was kept fresh by the observance of an annual fast. In some circles at least his name was remembered with respect.'

John's son, the new rightful king, Henry III, was but nine years old when his father died and appeared to be in a perilous position. He was under the protection of the Regent, the Earl of Pembroke. However, Louis was never popular with the rebel barons and it was not long before their alliance began to fall apart. Farnham Castle was retaken in the spring of 1217 but the Dauphin's forces at Guildford probably held out for some weeks longer. However, by September the war was over. The initial negotiations for peace were conducted at Kingston and from there, on 14th September, Louis was issued with what amounted to a safe conduct pass to enable him to leave England. His followers were granted the same safe conduct at Merton five days later. Thus there ended a series of important episodes in England's history in which the county of Surrey played no small part.

Trouble between the monarch and his barons festered through much of the reign of Henry III, who had a tendency to surround himself with crowds of foreign favourites. Matters came to a head during the 1260s, when a group of barons led by Simon de Montfort rose in rebellion. In 1264 the royal forces were routed by the barons at Lewes in Sussex, but a royal garrison based at Tonbridge succeeded in destroying Bletchingley Castle, the Surrey stronghold of the barons' ally, the Earl of Gloucester, who was the head of the de Clare family. Following their success at Lewes, de Montfort and his cronies met at the first English 'Parliament'. It was a far cry from our present democratic institution and had nothing to do with the rights of the common peasant. The following year Henry III and his son, the future Edward I, got their revenge at Evesham in Worcestershire, where de Montfort himself was slain.

It was during the reign of Henry III that Guildford Castle was developed into a royal palace. Today, apart from the 12th century keep, the arched entrance to the castle from Quarry Street and some isolated walls, nothing of the palace survives above ground. However, a series of archaeological 'digs' undertaken in recent years, coupled with

The entrance to Guildford Castle from an engraving of 1829. The arch was probably built by Henry III's master mason, John of Gloucester, in 1256.

detailed documentary research, have done much to shed light on life in the royal household in the 13th century. Excavation revealed a small section of the original outer bailey ditch which was filled in during the late 12th century. The considerably enlarged area of the bailey thus made available accommodated the extensive range of buildings required for such an important residence. There was the great hall, which was the centre of palace life – its remains now lie under two 19th century houses in Castle Hill. One called 'The Chestnuts' was the house where Alice's creator, Lewis Carroll, died in 1898.

Within the castle wall, close to the present Quarry Street, chambers were built for Henry's son, later Edward I, and for his queen, Eleanor. In 1990 archaeologists uncovered the remains of a building constructed of quality masonry. The dimensions of this important find exactly fitted the specifications for the building of 'Lord Edward's Chamber' as detailed in a surviving document of 1246. It was to be '50 ft long from the wall towards the street along the wall towards the field to the corner of the wall towards the kitchen . . . and 26 ft wide from the wall towards the field to almonry'. Parts of the foundations of the almonry, originally built in the 1220s and enlarged in 1238, were also discovered. The almoner had the job of collecting those revenues earmarked for charitable purposes.

A cesspit excavated in this area revealed amongst the rubbish deposited in it the fragments of a glass container known as a urinal. These vessels were used by medieval physicians to examine the urine of their patient. From its colour the physician would pronounce the state of the patient's health. It was tempting to link this discovery with the fatal illness of Lord Henry, the son of Edward I, who died at Guildford in 1274. Unfortunately, the connection was disproved by archaeologists because the cesspit had been filled in prior to the building of a new chamber for Queen Eleanor in 1268.

Queen Eleanor's original chamber was also built, like Lord Edward's, in 1246 and was probably situated to the east of the great hall. The new chamber was constructed adjacent to the almonry, and its remains have also been uncovered by archaeologists. Some of the substantial walls of the king's chambers can still be seen above ground in the south-west corner of the present Castle Gardens. At the entrance to Castle Hill is Castle Arch which was built in 1256 by the king's master mason, John of Gloucester, who carried out extensive work on the palace following a fire in 1254.

But what was life like for the commoners beyond the walls of this sumptuous royal palace? For most of Surrey's town dwellers the comparative peace of the reigns of Henry III and Edward I, brought increasing prosperity and expansion. Their markets flourished. Dorking's market was confirmed in 1278 and Haslemere certainly had a market by 1221, whilst Godalming's was confirmed by Edward I in 1300. The market at Leatherhead dates from a grant of Henry III in 1248 and at Farnham the Bishop of Winchester, Lord of the Manor, obtained the rights for a market in 1216. In 1249 the burgesses of Farnham were given their own charter of liberties making them responsible for running the affairs of the town separately from the manor. Reigate was founded as a new town by the de Warrennes at the gates of their castle. The original settlement of Cherchefelle, to the east, seems to have been abandoned apart from the church, which was retained on its original site. The new town's market was certainly thriving well before 1276. Most importantly, Guildford itself had developed as a major centre of woollen cloth manufacture and a charter of 1257 established this borough as the county town.

At Guildford, the townsman and their families lived in timber-framed houses fronting the High Street. Various trades and crafts were carried on in the houses and in the narrow strips of land behind them. Some strips had rights of way or 'gates' running between the properties, especially where inns and taverns developed. Several of these gates survive today, such as Tunsgate, Swan Lane (Swangate) and Market Street (formerly Red Lion Gate). In the late 13th century several High Street properties in Guildford were rebuilt and provided with semi-basement shops or 'undercrofts'. These stone-built vaulted cellars,

Farnham Fair in Castle Street in the 1880s – the town was first granted a market and fair in 1216.

with steps leading down from the street, were the result of the increasing demand for trade and shop premises. Two of these fascinating medieval structures still survive beneath more recent buildings. A similar stone undercroft has also been discovered in Kingston. As the borough of Guildford became more prosperous and pressure on building land increased, its houses were often rebuilt at right angles to the street in order to fit more properties into a single strip. The occupiers of these houses were the new growing breed of freemen – craftsmen, traders and entrepreneurs, often responsible to a guild but not tied to a lord's land.

However, the majority of Surrey's population still lived in a feudal society, toiling on their lord's land, whilst eking out a subsistence existence on the small plots allowed for their own crops. Some of them would have worked on small sub-manors like Alsted near Merstham, the site of which was rediscovered in the late 1960s. Here, archaeologists and historians have been able to reconstruct the story of a small manor house from the mid-13th century until its final abandonment at the beginning of the 15th century.

The first post-Conquest house on the Alsted site was built in the mid-13th century. A simple rectangular building measuring just over 28 × 13 ft, constructed of chalk, flint and local sandstone, roofed with clay tiles. It was probably a first floor hall, similar to those found in other parts of southern Britain. Unlike a number of similar establishments of the period, Alsted did not have a moat. Well over 100 such sites have, however, been identified in Surrey, mostly dating from the 13th and early 14th centuries. They were constructed with a square or rectangular water-filled moat surrounding the manor house.

At Tolworth, near Ewell, there are the scant remains of a moated manor house which belonged to Hugh le Despenser, a supporter of Edward II. After the unfortunate Hugh had been hanged when his worthless king was deposed in 1327, a survey was made of his property. The records show that within the moat at Tolworth there was a range of domestic buildings and a bakehouse, brewhouse and chapel. There

In 1278 Dorking's market was confirmed as having been in existence since 'time immemorial'. It continued in the High Street until 1926.

52

57493 Bletchingley, "Fair Day." Frith

Bletchingley Fair on 10th May 1907 – the first grant of a fair here was in 1283.

were also various agricultural buildings on the site, such as barns for the storage of grain, but these were all situated outside the moat. It is obvious from the position of these buildings that any defence of such a site would have been limited in its effectiveness. This has led most archaeologists to agree that these moats were constructed as a matter of status and fashion, rather than for any practical defensive reasons. The restoration of an undocumented moat at South Park, near Grayswood, was completed in 1994 and the site is now open to the public.

The simple unmoated manor house at Alsted was almost certainly the home of Ralph de Aldestede. Ralph's son, Robert, married a lady of substantial means, Sarah de Passele, and took her name. Thus the sub-manor passed to the de Passele, later Pashley, family. There is probably a link between this marriage and the rebuilding of the manor house along much more substantial lines in about 1270.

The new house had a timber-framed aisled hall, solar block and kitchen. Archaeologists found much evidence for iron working on the site throughout the period of occupation. There were also extensive indications around the site of the remains of the humble hovels of the tied workers of the manor's farming estate. It would have been a mixed farming economy with cattle, sheep and pigs, plus arable.

The manor house lay empty for 50 or 60 years following the death in 1341 of Margaret, wife of Edmund de Passele, son of Robert. Another reason for its desertion may have been the devastation wrought by the Black Death, which swept through England, including Surrey, following its arrival from the Continent in 1348. Then, for a brief period, Alsted was refurbished and much improved iron working facilities constructed. Finally, the place was abandoned to the brambles and nettles for more than 500 years. Left behind on the site were those many small possessions and everyday items of a medieval Surrey community which made life work – the broken pottery, mainly locally produced but including some fine ware imported from France, and metal objects such as keys, buckles and brooches. Perhaps most touching of all was the discovery of two clay marbles. Small matters that bring us so much closer to our medieval forebears.

7

FROM BLACK DEATH TO TUDOR TIMES

As with all of England, the Black Death must have come upon the county of Surrey like the approach of a storm. Firstly, with the increasing of the wind, came rumours of terrible death in somewhere far away. Then, there arrived the black clouds of terror, when those fleeing from the next village told of the strange pestilence which was carrying off their people. When the storm broke it was usually very sudden. The victim might be in perfect health at the start of a new day but, by evening, dead.

It is impossible to gauge how many in Surrey fell to the first visitation of the dread disease, which reached England from the Continent in 1348. The common assessment is for anything between a third and a half of the entire population of England, perhaps one to two million people out of a population of little over four million. There is no reason to suggest that in Surrey the proportion was any less. The plague was to come several times more before the century was out, but the first epidemic was undoubtedly the worst. The scant surviving records are usually of the religious houses – all the brethren of the hospital at Sandon, now Sandown near Esher, perished, as did the Prior of Reigate and the Abbot of Waverley. The records also show rapid and frequent changes in the local clergy at this time, certainly caused by the deaths of those who worked closest to the people.

The Black Death encouraged the break-up of the feudal system. The shortage of labour led to a scarcity of food and consequently to the offer of wages rather than service as a means of getting the farmwork done. Many villeins were freed from the obligation to work on the lord's land and paid a rent instead for their smallholdings. The government introduced the Statute of Labourers to control the situation and retain the status quo. It was an attempt to force labourers to remain working on their lord's land and for the same wages as before the plague. They were also forbidden from moving on in search of better wages elsewhere.

A later statute called for all apprehended labourers to be branded on the forehead with letter 'F' for falsity. These statutes proved unworkable.

In addition, whilst the country's fiscal requirements remained high during the Hundred Years War with France, the individual liability for tax, with the drastic drop in population, had considerably increased. The government dreamt up new taxes to raise its revenue. The Poll Tax was no more popular when reintroduced in the 1980s than it had been 600 years before. However, the consequences were somewhat more violent in 1381, when a third Poll Tax in four years raised the levy to one shilling for everyone over the age of 15.

The uprisings began, first in Kent and Essex, but they soon spread throughout much of the country, including Surrey. Particular targets were the manorial records and muniments which were the lord's evidence for the peasants' continuing bondage. The tenants of Chertsey stormed the Abbey and burnt some of its manorial rolls. A mob entered Guildford and destroyed the town's charter. A new charter was granted in 1384 because the originals had been 'lost' in 1381. As Surrey historian H.E. Malden wrote, 'The whole countryside was full of rapine, murder, and burnings, the outrages of an outraged peasantry, and the insurgents swarmed up towards London, where the Kentish men were already encamped upon Blackheath.'

On 12th June 1381 the rebels entered Southwark, where many of the local population joined forces with them. Marshalsea Prison was broken open and the prisoners liberated. The houses of 'obnoxious citizens' were destroyed along with the brothels, said to have been leased by the Bishop of Winchester to the Lord Mayor of London who made great profit from the women of Flanders who conducted their trade therein.

The following day the rebels were at the drawbridge of London Bridge where, according to John Stowe, the Surrey men 'cried to the warders of the bridge to let it down, whereby they might pass, or else they would destroy them all.' The warders duly let down the bridge to leave the city to its fate. Here the 14 year old King Richard II showed his mettle, riding out to face the rebels. At this meeting, Wat Tyler, the Kentish leader, insulted the King and was struck down by one of the noblemen. However, as H.E. Malden wrote so succinctly, 'the death of Wat Tyler, the courage of the young King and the strange melting away of the leaderless mob – belong to other history.'

Once matters had quietened down a little the aristocracy fell upon the peasants with the full force of their laws. Armies marched into Kent and Essex, where support for the revolt had been particularly strong. A commission was appointed for every county to deal heavily with offenders. A single commission for Surrey and Sussex was headed by the Earl of Arundel and Sir William Percy of Esher, the sheriff jointly for the two counties, plus five other 'gentlemen' from the two counties. So efficient was their work that it was not long before the county gaol at Guildford Castle, where the sheriff was based, was full and prisoners were taken to Arundel and Lewes.

Throughout these years of turmoil there were certain places in Surrey where a life of peace and relative tranquillity went on regardless. These places were, of course, the abbeys, priories and other religious establishments of the county. The chief amongst them was the Benedictine Abbey at Chertsey, founded, in AD 666. The abbey had suffered badly at the hands of the Danes during the 9th and 10th centuries but by the time of William's Conquest it had greatly recovered. In Domesday it is listed as the holder of extensive lands in the county. In 1110 a major programme of rebuilding was begun by Abbot Hugh and this work probably continued for most of that century. A serious fire damaged the monastic buildings in 1235, requiring further rebuilding under Abbot Alan who died in 1261. In July 1370 a calamity befell the abbey church when 'the central part of the bell tower fell to the ground to the irrecoverable damage of the house' – a matter recorded in the Chertsey Abbey cartularies. In 1471 King Henry VI was buried at the abbey and, until his body was removed to Windsor in 1484, the abbey became a place of pilgrimage.

The Cistercian Abbey of Waverley, the first of its order in England, was founded near Tilford by William Gillard, Bishop of Winchester, in 1128. The Cistercians took their name from their chief abbey at Cîteaux (Cistercium in Latin) in Burgundy, but the monks who established Waverley came from Aumone in Normandy. The order was founded by an Englishman, Stephen Harding, who led a movement away from what he considered to be the worldliness of the Benedictines or Black Monks. The rules of Harding's 'White Monks' were severe and included a rule stating that 'none of our houses are to be built in cities, in castles, or villages, but in places remote from the conversation of men, and let all churches of our order be dedicated and founded in honour of the Blessed Mary.' Thus their houses, like Fountains Abbey or Tintern, were usually built in quiet riverside locations.

The original buildings at Waverley were very small but, during the late 12th and throughout much of the 13th century, the abbey was gradually rebuilt on a much grander scale. By 1187 it had a number of daughter houses, including Thame in Oxfordshire and Garendon in Leicestershire. There were 70 monks and 120 lay brothers in the monastery at this time. Waverley's chief contribution to the local communities of west Surrey was the introduction of the wool trade. The

Waverley Abbey was the first Cistercian monastery in England and was founded in 1128.

abbey possessed several thousand sheep producing fleeces of the finest quality which attracted buyers from the Low Countries, France and Italy. It is known to have supplied the Florentines with wool in 1315. On several occasions the more entrepreneurial of the monks landed the abbey in debt when they over-estimated the future price of wool.

The monks of Waverley are also thought to have been responsible for the building of a series of bridges over the river Wey downstream of their abbey in the late 13th century. Remarkably, several of these bridges have survived, including two at Tilford, where the two branches of the river meet, and, perhaps the best example, at Eashing, upstream of Godalming, which is in effect also two bridges crossing the main river and the millstream.

Today, the ruins of Waverley Abbey still stand in a tranquil setting beside the clear waters of the river Wey against a backdrop of wooded hills. We can still appreciate the beauty of the place just as the first monks must have done when they arrived here from Normandy nearly 900 years ago.

There were several monastic houses in Surrey belonging to the Canons Regular of St Augustine or Austin Canons as they were more usually known. The most important of these was at Merton, but there were others at Reigate, Tandridge and near Ripley. The canons were ordained priests who lived strictly by the rules of St Augustine of Hippo. Theirs were not, however, closed houses built for peaceful seclusion like those of the Cistercians, but places which provided many benefits to the lay people beyond their walls. In particular, they gave lodging, food and care to the aged sick and also offered schooling for the boys of the area.

Most of their establishments contained only a small number of canons, who worked closely with their local communities. They would often be seen in the town or village, always clad in their characteristic long black cassock, with a shorter white surplice over the top of the cassock. They also wore a long, black cloak fastened at the neck. Most distinctive of all was the four sided black cap, often set on the head at a rather jaunty angle. This was despite the fact that one of the rules stipulated that members of the order should '. . . not be remarked by their habit, not endeavour to please by their clothing, but by their behaviour. The head and hair be covered and carefully arranged.' Prayers every three hours, day and night, were an obvious burden to the canons as were the periods of fasting. In between times their 'frugal' diet, which, according to Alfred Heales writing in the 19th century, consisted of 'herbs, eggs, fish, bread, cheese, butter and ale or beer', would, perhaps, have been the envy of the average Surrey peasant.

The ruins of Newark Priory, founded during the reign of Richard I in the late 12th century, still stand in a beautiful setting on the banks of the

THE RUINS OF NEWARK PRIORY 13TH CENTURY.

Newark Priory was founded during the reign of Richard I in the late 12th century.

river Wey near Ripley. Tandridge was a small priory with perhaps no more than five canons. Originally established in the second half of the 13th century as the Hospital of St James, it had become an Augustinian priory by the early years of the following century.

Reigate Priory was founded by William de Warrenne, sixth Earl of Surrey, in about 1235, close to the de Warrenne 'new town'. The arrangement of its buildings was typical of many such establishments. At the heart of the priory was the church, which was also open to the townspeople, who were separated from the prior and canons by the rood screen between the nave and the choir. The priory church became so popular as a place of worship for the people of Reigate that they neglected their parish church. The priory church was obviously more convenient, being closer to the town. In 1374, the Bishop of Winchester forbade parishoners from attending services such as mass at the priory church to the detriment of their own church. The penalty for disobeying the bishop, that of excommunication, was never a matter to be taken lightly in those days.

To one side of the church was the outer court with its offices, stables and stores and the hospitium or guest house for the boarding of visitors. These buildings were usually on the north side, whilst to the south of the church were the cloisters surrounding the garden, and the chapter house, kitchens, dormitories and infirmary. Reigate Priory, like most monastic sites, was situated adjacent to a stream to provide a good supply of clean water. The stream could also be dammed to provide lakes and ponds for the fish which were an important part of the monks' diet.

The important priory at Merton was rather older than Reigate, having been founded in 1114. St Thomas à Becket was educated there and also Walter de Merton, Chancellor of England, who founded Merton College, Oxford. The canons at Merton certainly knew how to enjoy life, particularly hunting, a pursuit specifically forbidden to them. In 1387 the Bishop of Winchester had to write to the canons to remind them that the keeping of hunting dogs within the precincts of the priory was strictly prohibited. Any canon caught ignoring this rule was liable to be restricted to merely bread and ale for six feast days.

Hunting was, of course, the first love of most of the medieval kings of England, who were constantly seeking ways to extend their forest rights. Surrey, situated on London's doorstep, with the Royal Forest of Windsor to the north-west, was particularly popular, especially with Henry II. He afforested his own lands in Surrey, including Guildford and Woking, linking them to Windsor. Finally, he attempted to include the whole of the county under Forest Law. There were reasons for this other than the pure love of the chase. Forest Law, through its courts, increased

The late 13th century bridge at Eashing was probably built by the monks of Waverley Abbey.

royal power over and above that of the barons and clergy. Only the king could own the forest and within it all rights were subservient to those of the monarch. Apart from the stringent protection of game, a royal licence was needed to cut wood and tolls might be charged for the right of passage through the forest. Most significant for the peasant was that Forest Law made it a grave offence to grub up trees, or 'assart', to make land fit for the cultivation of crops. All fines, rents and tolls collected at these courts went straight to the king.

Thus, the extension of the royal forests was a constant source of friction between the barons and their king. Amongst the many demands pressed on King John at Runnymede was that he deforest large areas of the country afforested by him and his predecessors. In 1226 Henry III gave up his forest rights in Surrey in return for a large subsidy. This in effect removed Forest Law from the county, except for the king's own park at Guildford, and restricted Windsor Forest to the Berkshire side of the county boundary.

The intermittent turmoil of the Wars of the Roses, as Yorkists and Lancastrians fought for the supremacy of England, seems hardly to have touched the county of Surrey. Ironically, it was the Tudor king, Henry VII, who in the last years of the 15th century emerged as the unopposed ruler of a united country. Unopposed, that is, except in a distant and almost forgotten corner of his domain, Cornwall. Here, rebellion was aroused in 1497 by the swingeing taxes imposed by Henry to finance his wars with the Scots – a remarkable tale that links the Cornish rebels to Guildford, the county town of Surrey.

In Henry VII's time most of the Cornish people were still Celtic, with a culture and language which could be traced back to before the coming of the Romans. It was natural that they should feel resentment when asked to make heavy contributions to a war being conducted in a foreign country hundreds of miles away. The rebels were led by a blacksmith, Michael Joseph, from St Keverne on the Lizard peninsula. A rebel 'army', said to be 15,000 strong, gathered at Bodmin in May 1497, and began the long protest march towards London. They were poorly armed, for bloodshed was not their true intention and a direct battle against the king seemed far from their minds. Prominent amongst them was a Bodmin lawyer, Thomas Flamank, whose criticisms were not directed at the king but at two of Henry's councillors and closest advisors, Cardinal Morton and Sir Reginald Bray, whose landholdings included the Manor of Shere Vachery in Surrey. It was Flamank's assertion that the taxes were illegal and that Cornishmen could bring about a just settlement without recourse to destruction and murder. As Francis Bacon put it succinctly, 'he could tell how to make rebellion and never break the peace.'

Unfortunately, the rebels got only as far as Taunton before a murder was committed, that of a tax commissioner, but this event invoked no retaliation from the men of Somerset, who no doubt had their own views about the worthiness of such men. At Wells the Cornishmen were joined by the only man of rank to show open support for their cause – James Touchet, the seventh Baron Audley, who was the Lord of the main Manor of Shere. We can only guess at his motives but he was to remain true to the cause until the end.

The rebels swept across southern England without meeting any opposition. They had hoped that the men of Kent, whose reputation for open rebellion against injustice went back to the days of Wat Tyler and the Peasants' Revolt, would swell their numbers. In this they were to be disappointed and few, if any, from that county were prepared to throw in their lot with them. London was the rebels' goal, which brought them into Surrey and on Tuesday, 13th June 1497, they encamped on the outskirts of Guildford, probably on Guildown.

We have no idea how the people of Guildford greeted this motley band of rebels, who must have outnumbered them by at least fifteen to one. They seem to have kept their distance for there are no records showing Guildford men amongst the rebels' complement. Equally, there are no records of any confrontation between the rebels and the inhabitants, who may at least have provided the Cornishmen with provisions.

Meanwhile, Henry VII was in no mood to receive a Cornish petition and began to muster his troops for battle. He already had an army of 8,000 men under Lord Daubeney ready for the Scottish war. On Wednesday, 14th June, Daubeney sent out a detachment of 500 mounted spearmen to seek out the enemy. By some accounts they came upon the rebels by accident and, on the hill above Guildford, a brief but bloody battle ensued. Daubeney's force made a tactical retreat having taken prisoners and determined the mettle of the Cornishmen.

The rebels now finally moved towards London, their resolve perhaps dented by the incident at Guildford. On the afternoon of Friday, 16th June, they arrived within sight of London and made camp on Blackheath. By this time Henry had gathered further forces and now had 25,000 men standing in defence of his capital. He surprised the Cornishmen early the following morning but, by all reports, the rebels initially gave a good account of themselves. Three hundred royal troops were killed by the Cornish archers and Daubeney himself taken prisoner for a short while. However, it was inevitable that Henry's trained troops would soon prevail and the Cornishmen were routed, fleeing the battlefield in disarray, their leaders captured. Henry crossed London Bridge early that afternoon to be received in triumph by the Mayor and the loyal burghers of the capital.

On 27th June 1497, Michael Joseph and Thomas Flamank were taken from the Tower to Tyburn where they were hanged, drawn and quartered. Audley, as befitted a nobleman, was taken the next day from Newgate to Tower Hill, wearing 'a cote armour upon hym of papir, all to torne', and there beheaded. Sir Reginald Bray had been one of the main targets of the rebels' wrath. It was, perhaps, no coincidence that the unfortunate Audley's lordship of Shere passed to the Bray family, where it resides to this day.

8

THE EARLY TUDORS

In the reign of Henry VIII the power of the monarchy reached its zenith. It was a time, wrote Surrey historian H.E. Malden, when 'the personal will of the Crown became the directing force whereby everything was determined'. As Henry VIII's reign progressed his increasingly corpulent figure seemed to cast an ever-larger shadow over the lives of all his people. In Surrey his power was felt perhaps more than in most other shires.

His love of hunting and the chase made Henry look with eagerness at the prospects for his sport in the Surrey countryside so close to London. By exchanges or confiscation, and occasionally by purchase, he acquired a block of manors in Surrey, including Byfleet, Weybridge, Walton, Oatlands near Weybridge, Molesey, Esher and Malden, and declared them royal forest. It was, therefore, only natural that he should wish to have close by the chase a residence or two fit for a very special king.

On 12th October 1537 Henry's long awaited son, Edward, was born to his third wife, Jane Seymour. The succession of the Tudor dynasty was now assured and in celebration Henry decided to embark on the building of a major new palace. This palace was to be better than anything Henry's rival, Francis I of France, had at Fontainebleau. It would be built to the glory of the Tudors and no expense would be spared. It would have no equal; there would be 'none such' anywhere in the world – it was Nonsuch Palace.

The site for this new wonder was chosen for its open countryside with excellent hunting, its clean air and its good supply of pure water. The palace was to be built at Cuddington, between Ewell and Cheam. It was near to Hampton Court, Henry's extensive palace across the Thames in Middlesex and thus was also within easy reach of London by boat down the Thames. To the south was Banstead Downs and in all there were at least 40 square miles of country suitable for the hunting of almost everything that moved – deer, fox, badger, pheasant, partridge, 'coney' and 'all kinds of vermin'. The fact that this ideal site had a complete village, including a manor house and church, situated on it was not, of course, any deterrent to the king.

Joris Hoefnagel's view of Nonsuch Palace in 1582. The site of the palace was rediscovered and excavated in 1959

The Lord of the Manor of this village was Sir Richard Codington and his manor house was described by Henry's surveyors as 'newly built'. From the description it appears to have been a typical manor house of the period, with a great hall, ample living quarters for the Codingtons, a kitchen and servants' quarters, all built round three sides of a rectangle. The church at Cuddington belonged to the powerful priory at Merton but even that did not stop Henry in his determination to remove it. Just one week before the building of Nonsuch Palace commenced at Cuddington, Merton Priory was dissolved.

Henry's closure of England's religious houses has been claimed by many historians to have been an act of pure vandalism – a despotic king and his crony, Thomas Cromwell, driven by avarice to destroy the religious houses and take all their riches for themselves. There can be no doubt that the monastic movement had lost its way by the start of the 16th century. The secular had in many cases taken over from the religious and many houses had become nothing more than businesses, their abbots or priors working closely with the local gentry for the maximum profit to both. Many of the lucrative lay jobs associated with the monasteries were an inheritance for the gentry, whose ancestors had often been responsible for the founding of the establishments in the first place. As centres of learning, the monasteries had declined and the invention of printing had made their scribes redundant. On the other hand, there were still those religious houses whose inmates spoke the word of God before all else and whose efforts for the charity of others cannot be doubted. But it was the time for change and the King was leading a reformation with much support from his people, especially those who saw a chance for personal gain.

The first wave of closures commenced in 1536, when all religious houses worth under £200 a year were dissolved and 'converted to better uses'. In Surrey this first round of closures included Tandridge and Reigate priories. At Tandridge the end came on 2nd July 1536, when the canons were dispersed and the prior paid off with a pension of £14 per annum. Reigate Priory was rated at only £68 16s 10d and its prior received a pension of £10. In 1541 Henry granted Reigate Priory to Lord William Howard, eldest son of Thomas Howard, Duke of Norfolk and Earl of Surrey. The priory was to remain in Howard family ownership until 1681 and over the years was altered into a country seat. Most of its buildings gradually disappeared but the priory church was converted into the main dwelling and part of its medieval fabric still survives in the present Reigate Priory, which is now a school.

The important Cistercian abbey at Waverley also fell victim to the first round of closures. Its fortunes were already in decline by the time Henry's commissioners visited it, clearly with an eye on finding reason for suppression. Not surprisingly, they reported that the fewer than 30 monks left in the house were disorderly and dissolute. The abbot, William Ayling, was described as 'honest but none of the children of Solomon' and 'every monk was his own master'. When the end came the monks were turned out to find a living as best they could. One of them, John Parker, became curate of Wanborough, where the chapel there had previously been attached to the abbey. Compared with the priors of Reigate and Tandridge, Abbot Ayling was granted a generous pension of £70 a year. He went to Oxford to become provost of what is now St John's College. He also held a living at Froxall in Staffordshire, so he was not exactly left in dire straits by the closure of his abbey. Perhaps some of the criticism of the lavish lifestyle of some of the monks of this period is borne out by the details of Abbot Ayling's will in 1539. His bequests included no less than three feather beds and a large and costly wardrobe. Not bad for a leader of an order whose founders had rejected all forms of luxury and wealth!

The act which brought about the demise of Tandridge, Reigate and Waverley did not include the more valuable houses, the 'great and solemn monasteries wherein (thanks be to God) religion is right well kept and observed'. But the sincerity in these words was false and only a matter of administrative expediency – within four years all the religious houses had gone. Chertsey Abbey surrendered on 6th July 1537 but, curiously, King Henry proposed to re-establish the monks at Bisham only to have Bisham itself dissolved eleven months later.

The Dominican friary at Guildford, founded in the 13th century, closed its doors on 15th October 1538. It had played host to many royal visitors through the centuries – following a visit by Henry IV in 1403 the friary received compensation of 40 shillings for damage caused by the royal entourage. Even as late as 1534 a treaty with Scotland was ratified at Guildford Friary and there is evidence to suggest that rebuilding took place after this date. During 1535 '35 loads of tymber [were] caryed into the freyers at Guldeford' during the construction of a 'new buyldyng'. But all this was to no avail. After closure the friary remained in royal hands, parts of it being demolished and the rest being converted into a house.

By 1605 the friary was in ruins and it was demolished soon after, eventually making way for a fine mansion built by John Murray, Viscount Annandale, about 1610. Later the site became the home of the famous Friary Brewery. Prior to its redevelopment as a shopping precinct in the late 1970s, the site was extensively excavated by archaeologists. They revealed a wealth of remains, including substantial foundations, which enabled the reconstruction of an almost complete ground plan of the friary. Everything was then destroyed, as is the way with modern building techniques, leaving just a name, 'The Friary', to remind the future of its past.

Apart from those monastic buildings converted for domestic use, many were despoiled immediately following suppression. Their buildings were stripped of lead roofs and other valuable materials and then quarried for their stone. In 1538 the broken remains of medieval carvings from Chertsey Abbey were amongst the stones carted to Weybridge, where Henry was building his new palace of Oatlands on the site of a manor house previously owned by William Rede, a London goldsmith. As Henry just happened to be in possession of Tandridge Priory at the time, Rede was given it in exchange – a poor swop for a house placed handily near the Thames. Merton Priory, Surrey's most valuable religious house at the time of its suppression, suffered a similar fate to Chertsey, for just a few miles down the road at Cuddington, Henry had embarked on the building of Nonsuch.

It was during the reign of Henry VIII's father that Surrey had once more become an important royal home, in a way not seen since the medieval days of Henry III at Guildford. Admittedly, the royal manor at Sheen, on the banks of the Thames, had always been popular with a succession of kings. Edward III died there, as did Richard II's queen, Anne of Bohemia. Richard was so upset by her death that he had the

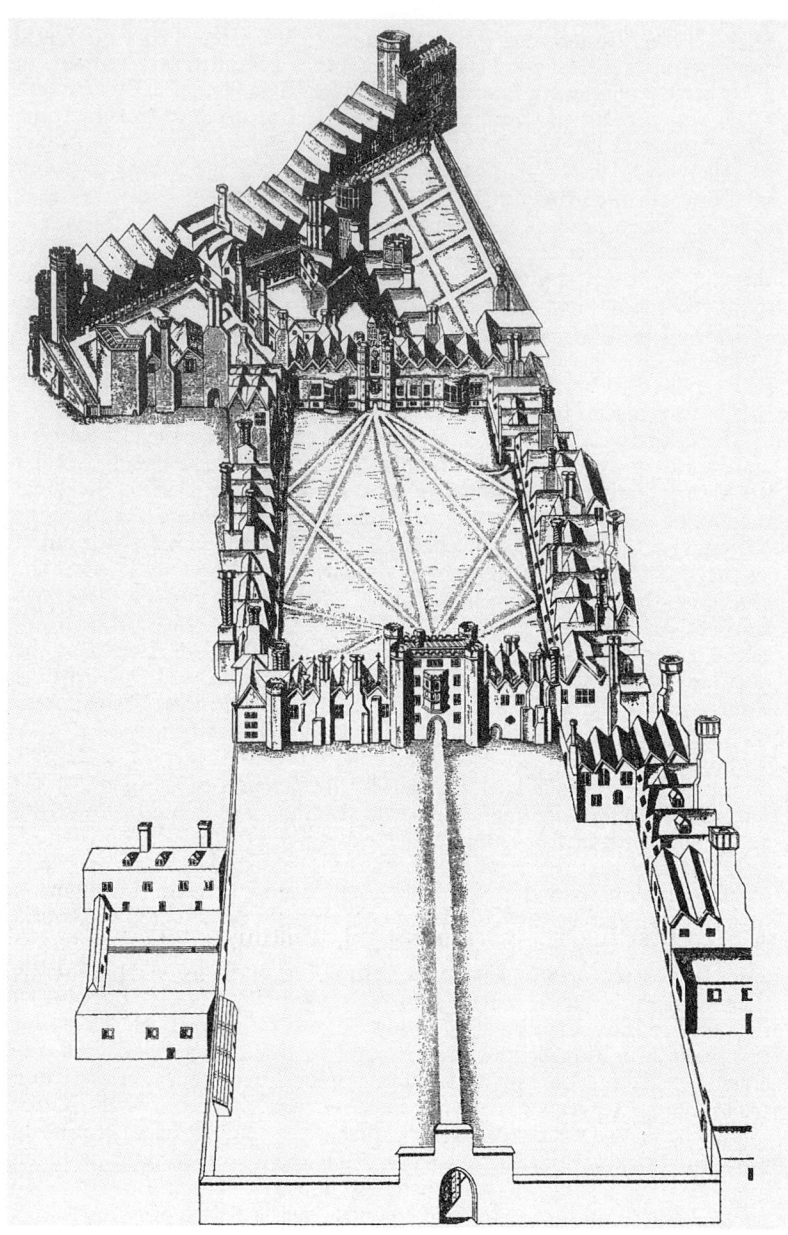

Oatlands Palace near Weybridge in Elizabeth I's reign.

place pulled down. Then Henry V rebuilt it, but it was Henry VII who reconstructed it as a magnificent royal palace fit for the founder of the Tudor dynasty. He called his new palace Richmond, after the earldom he had held before becoming king. Richmond soon supplanted Sheen as the name for the adjacent town which had grown up around it.

The palaces at Richmond and also at Hampton Court consisted of ranges of domestic buildings round two courtyards. The outer court was provided with a substantial gatehouse with octagonal turrets. A smaller but taller gatehouse led from the outer court to the inner court. This was the basic Tudor palace design adopted by the unknown architects of Henry VIII's new palaces in Surrey – Oatlands at Weybridge and, the finest of them all, Nonsuch. What made Nonsuch stand out above all the dozen or so palaces which Henry already possessed was the lavishness of its external decoration.

The walls of the inner court, two polygonal towers and the south facing outer wall of the palace were covered with an incredible decoration of carved and gilded slate and pure dazzling white stucco reliefs. Much of this work is thought to have been executed by a team of French craftsmen led by an Italian, Nicholas Bellin. Henry had managed to poach Bellin from his arch-rival, Francis I of France, for whom Bellin had worked at Fontainebleau. The stucco reliefs within the inner court included huge figures of gods and goddesses and figures representing the labours of Hercules, with above them busts of Roman emperors. Opposite the entrance to the court were the imposing figures of Henry himself, and his son, Prince Edward. On the outside south wall there were figures from Ovid's *Metamorphoses*. Further decoration around all these deeply recessed reliefs consisted of royal arms, mottoes, animals, cherubs, angels and garlands of fruit and flowers. The medium, known as stucco duro, consisted of a mixture of flint and chalk, crushed and burnt, mixed with water, which when dry became as hard as stone. It dried quickly and therefore the artist had to work at speed, building up the layers of stucco and moulding the reliefs using bare hands as well as special tools. When dry, the reliefs were whitewashed to increase their awesome effect. This was Henry's intention – to let the world know that his great Tudor dynasty was the equal of gods and emperors.

The gardens at Nonsuch were laid out with a plethora of statuary and fountains on a scale to match the grandeur of the palace itself. There was a privy garden with a formal arrangement of small flowering plants – violets, primroses, sweet williams, wallflowers and roses, and herbs such as rosemary and thyme. A fountain of Venus was raised up on a small mound as the centrepiece. Throughout the gardens there were trees such as oak, elm, yew, cypress, bay and holly as well as a large variety of fruit trees – pear, apple, cherry and even apricot. Gardeners were sent all over Europe to bring back the latest varieties. There was a maze, a grove dedicated to the goddess, Diana, and a trick pyramid which cascaded water over the unsuspecting visitor who happened to tread on a particular paving stone.

Nonsuch had two parks – the Little Park adjacent to the palace, which included the 16 acres of gardens, and the Great Park of over 900 acres, stocked with deer for the hunt. Later known as Worcester Park after the Earl who was appointed keeper there in 1606, a substantial part of the Great Park was developed into housing estates during the present century, and covered with rows of mock-Tudor villas typical of 1930s suburban sprawl.

Surrey is fortunate that, despite the pressures of modern development, many genuine houses of all shapes and sizes have survived from the 15th and 16th centuries. Four miles north of Guildford is Sutton Place, one of the finest Tudor Renaissance houses to have survived anywhere in England. It was built in the 1520s by Sir Richard Weston, a Knight of the Bath and a Gentleman of the Privy Chamber, who later became Under-Treasurer of England. Weston was a born survivor during a reign when to be close to the centre of power brought riches but also personal danger. His son was executed as one of the supposed lovers of Anne Boleyn, but Sir Richard remained in favour and died a natural death in 1542. He built his house in brick and terracotta, the latter being used not only for moulded decoration but also for those dressings more usually done in stone, such as string courses, mullions, turrets, arches and parapets. Sutton Place was originally nearly square, the ranges of rooms on two storeys being built round a courtyard. In 1786 the north side, which included the main gatehouse, was demolished. But what remains was described by architectural writer Ian Nairn as 'side by side with Layer Marney [in Essex], the most important English house of the years following immediately after Hampton Court'.

For the majority of houses of the period, however, wood was the main construction material. Stout oak timbers from the local forests were chosen for a timber frame, which was usually infilled with wattle and daub, but later brick or stone was also used. There was very little thatching done in Surrey and clay tiles or stone slates were the norm to roof these timber-framed houses. Thanks to the work of the Domestic Buildings Research Group of Surrey during the last 20 years, several thousand old houses have been surveyed and recorded throughout Surrey. The oldest, such as that discovered in Hart's Yard, Godalming, date in part to pre-1400.

The earliest houses in Surrey to survive substantially intact are 15th century. They originally consisted of a central hall, open to the roof with first floor rooms fitted under the slope of the roof. Smoke from the open fire would simply drift upwards and eventually find an exit through small openings at either end of the building. Life in these houses, especially in winter, must have been lived in a smoke-filled

Brewer Street Farmhouse, Bletchingley, which was built in the 15th century.

haze and such buildings today can be recognised by their smoke-blackened roof timbers. Puttenden Manor near Lingfield and Brewer Street Farmhouse at Bletchingley are good examples of this style of building. The latter is roofed with stone tiles known as Horsham slates from a natural stone quarried in various places in the Weald, which has cleaving properties similar to slate.

By about 1500, to increase the number of rooms and to solve the smoke problem, some houses in Surrey were constructed with extra flooring over part of the open hall. Some existing houses were also given this addition. The flooring provided more bedroom space upstairs and left only one bay of the hall open to the roof. This meant that the smoke was more quickly drawn out and did not linger to permeate every nook and cranny of the house. Over 50 houses with this suspended upper floor have so far been recognised in the county, a good example being Saplings in Newdigate.

After about 1550, houses were constructed with framing specifically designed with only one small bay open to the roof above the hearth. Side draughts were eliminated, thus leading to easier control of the smoke,

Sutton Place near Woking was built by Sir Richard Weston in the 1520s.

which quickly made its exit via a wattle hood in the roof. Larger houses had the smoke bay in the middle but in the smaller cottage it was built at one end. There are numerous examples of these 'smoke bay houses' to be found in Surrey, for the design continued into the early 17th century. Meanwhile, about 1580, came the introduction of chimneys, solidly built in brick or stone. They were an obvious development from the small smoke bay which, over the following 50 years, they replaced.

Timber-frame building in oak did not entirely die out with the widespread introduction of brick and stone in the second part of the 17th century. Until well into the Georgian period the style was still used, but these small cottages are debased examples, poorly constructed, with joints held together with iron nails, like some still to be seen at Hurtmore near Godalming. Following on from this sad end to an ancient craft, came a completely new style of framing using soft woods, which were then protected from the elements by weather-boarding. This type of house or cottage was more commonly found in north-east Surrey, where a few still survive.

9

ELIZABETHAN SURREY

Henry VIII died in 1547, leaving Nonsuch unfinished. Despite his initial enthusiasm and the vast expense, he had stayed there only rarely. Other more pressing matters deflected him and his declining health curtailed his pursuit of hunting. His search for an adequate replacement for his much lamented Jane Seymour had led him into an unfortunate attachment to Anne of Cleves. His chief minister, Thomas Cromwell, persuaded Henry of her supposed beauty via a flattering portrait drawn by Holbein. In reality she was very plain indeed and it required all of Cromwell's guile to force the marriage through. Henry was soon confiding to Sir Anthony Denny of his Privy Chamber 'How he would utter plainly to him, as to a servant whom he used secretly about him, . . . that he could never . . . be provoked and stirred to know her carnally'. Thus the marriage was annulled. The episode brought Thomas Cromwell's head to the block but Anne did not share the same fate. Henry had no real argument with her and, more importantly, she had powerful allies abroad. He offered her quiet retirement, which she was happy to accept. She became the Lady of the Manor of Bletchingley.

Henry's son, Edward VI, was a sickly boy whose short reign ended before his 16th birthday. When Henry's daughter, the Catholic Mary, came to the throne, intrigue and revolution were expected. In the event, the only serious rising came from a force led by Thomas Wyatt. He threatened London from the south but, just like many before him, he failed to take London Bridge. Wyatt finally crossed the Thames by Kingston Bridge, which at the time was the first bridge upstream from the capital, but on approaching London most of his force melted away, leaving their leader to feeble surrender and the inevitable consequences of his actions.

There was an attempt to implicate Thomas Cawarden, Anne of Cleves' keeper at Bletchingley, in this plot to remove Mary. Cawarden was arrested and a large arsenal of weapons, which he had accumulated at his house, Place House in Bletchingley, were confiscated. The weapons

Anne of Cleves, who became Lady of the Manor of Bletchingley after her marriage to Henry VIII had been annulled.

included 16 cannon and enough arms and equipment for a force of some 100 horsemen and over 300 foot soldiers. It must be remembered that at this period there was no standing army in England, and the shires could be called upon at short notice to provide a force for the defence of the realm. This was undoubtedly the reason Cawarden gave for being in possession of these arms. The authorities chose to believe him and he was soon released, complaining for some time afterwards that the contents of his arsenal had not been returned.

Queen Mary seems to have had little time for Nonsuch Palace and threatened to have it demolished, but in the end she sold it to the Earl of Arundel. Following Mary's death in 1558, Arundel bankrupted himself completing Henry's masterpiece, in the vain notion that Queen Elizabeth might be flattered into marrying him. However, Elizabeth was less impressed by Arundel's attentions than she was by Nonsuch. She loved the place – so much so that she often stayed there. When Arundel died in 1579 Nonsuch passed to his son-in-law, Lord Lumley. His expensive tastes meant that, just like his father-in-law, he was perennially in debt and in 1591 he passed the ownership of Nonsuch to Elizabeth. Lumley continued to live at Nonsuch as the Queen's Keeper, an arrangement which suited them both admirably.

Most of Elizabeth's time seems to have been taken up in progresses from one palace to another, or from one of her subject's houses to another. As the Earl of Arundel found out whenever she came to Nonsuch, it was a very expensive business entertaining the monarch and her huge retinue. She was frequently in Surrey – staying at Richmond, Oatlands or, just across the river from Surrey, at Hampton Court. She also stayed at Loseley, the seat of Sir William More between Godalming and Guildford, at Sutton Place where she was entertained by the Westons, and at several other lesser houses in the county. Despite the expense, her subjects vied with each other for the right to entertain their queen. Following a stay of one night at Mitcham, the owner of the house, Sir Julius Caesar, wrote, 'the Queen visited my house at Mitcham and

It was at Kingston Bridge that rebels led by Thomas Wyatt crossed the Thames on their way to London and their futile attempt to remove the Catholic Queen Mary

supped and lodged there, and dined there the next day. I presented her with a gown of cloth of silver richly embroidered; a black network mantle with pure gold, a taffeta hat, white with several flowers, and a jewel of gold set therein with rubies and diamonds. Her Majesty removed from my house after dinner the 13th of September to Nonsuch with exceeding good contentment; which entertainment of Her Majesty . . . amounted to £700 besides my own provisions and what was sent unto me by my friends.'

For each move she made, even the less well-off of her people were likely to incur expense, when their horses and carts were requisitioned as transport for the chattels of the court. When Jacob Rathgeb, secretary to the Duke of Wurttemberg, visited England in 1592 he noted that 'When the Queen breaks up her Court with the intention of visiting another place, there commonly follow more than three hundred carts laden with bag and baggage.' The repeated movement of the court not only enabled the queen to maintain a high profile amongst her subjects, but it also had practical purposes. With a large retinue of rarely washed

The remains of the gatehouse of Blechingley Place were converted into a farmhouse in the early 18th century.

courtiers within a confined space, the air must have quickly become most foul, especially with the garderobes and privies full to overflowing. The court moved on, leaving others to clean up the mess. And then there was always the threat of plague. The queen was at Windsor at the end of September 1563 when the disease struck the area around Reading and Newbury. With hundreds of people dying, plans were made to separate her from her retinue, who might become a source of infection and '. . . if her Highness shall be forced to move, as God forbid, I think then best the Household shall be put on board wages . . . and herself repair to Oatlands, where Her Majesty may remain well if no great resort be made to the house', wrote the Marquis of Winchester to Sir William Cecil, Elizabeth's chief minister.

Just like her father, Elizabeth loved the chase and it was principally for hunting that the court came to Oatlands. John Selwyn, Keeper of the Park at Oatlands, was credited with a remarkable feat of huntsmanship during one such visit – the event is depicted on a brass in nearby Walton church, where he was buried in 1587. Whilst chasing a stag on horseback, in full view of the queen, he managed to get alongside the unfortunate beast and leapt from his mount onto its back. He then, with the aid of his sword, guided the stag to Elizabeth and killed it at her feet.

Elizabeth was often at Nonsuch in the summer and it was here in 1599 that Thomas Platter, a German, and his party were allowed entry to the 'presence chamber' to view the queen and her court. The visitors were first impressed by the magnificent tapestries which adorned the walls within the palace. Platter noted that within the chamber the floor was 'strewn with straw or hay, only where the queen was to come out and up to her seat were carpets laid down worked in Turkish knot'. The entry of Queen Elizabeth was preceded by a number of men from the inner chamber carrying white staffs, followed by a large group of lords. When the queen herself entered she came in alone 'without escort, very straight and erect', wrote Platter. 'She was most lavishly attired in a gown of pure white satin, gold embroidered, with a whole bird of paradise for panache, set forward on her head studded with costly jewels; she wore a string of huge pearls about her neck and elegant gloves over which were drawn costly rings. In short she was most gorgeously apparelled, . . . she was very youthful still in appearance, seeming no more than twenty years of age. She had a dignified and regal bearing.' Platter was perhaps a little overawed by the whole event to suggest that the queen looked only 20 – she was in fact 66!

After listening to a sermon from 'a preacher in a white surplice, merely standing on the floor facing the Queen', Elizabeth withdrew again into the inner chamber. It was now time for the midday meal, the arrival of which was preceded by the entry of a large number of guards and courtiers, all of whom bowed three times as they came into the chamber. Tables were put before the throne, which was decorated with red damask embroidered with gold with low cushions beneath a great ornate canopy fixed to the ceiling. The tables were laid and then there entered a procession of 'tall, fine young men', dressed in red tabards, each of whom carried a dish of food. '. . . I observed amongst them some very large joints of beef, and all kinds of game, pastries and tarts', Platter recorded. The carving of the meat was done by a lady-in-waiting and portions were then taken in to Elizabeth who '. . . ate of what she fancied, privily however, for she very seldom partakes before strangers.' The meal lasted three courses, but Platter and his friends were not offered any. Afterwards '. . . musicians appeared in the Presence Chamber with their trumpets and shawms, and after they had performed their music, everyone withdrew, bowing themselves out just as they had come in, and the tables were carried away again.' The hungry Germans were finally given a meal in a tent outside before touring the gardens.

Not all Englishmen in Elizabeth's reign could rely on their next meal, for it was a time of widely differing fortunes for her people as a whole. Those with land prospered and a whole new class of independent yeoman farmers came into being. The growing population of London brought wealth to Surrey's farmers and landowners as the capital became the chief market for their produce. For the lords and gentry all the trappings of a comfortable life were easily at hand. Food was cheap and plentiful and there were riches to be made in the trading of commodities such as wool and cloth. Amongst Surrey's towns, Guildford and Godalming prospered greatly as centres of woollen cloth manufacture during Elizabeth's reign.

But for the poor these were hard times indeed. For those many thousands who found themselves unable to share in the new prosperity there was only charity to save them. The principal benefactor to the poor of Surrey was undoubtedly Henry Smith, who was born in Wandsworth, at that time in Surrey, in 1548. He became a very wealthy silversmith and City of London alderman who gave generously to most of the towns of the county during his lifetime. When he died in 1627, the bulk of his fortune was left in trust to provide for the poor of parishes throughout Surrey.

An unconfirmed tale has Smith as an old man walking from village to village along the tracks and byways of Surrey, disguised as a beggar, accompanied only by his faithful dog. The level of his later generosity was supposedly based upon the treatment which he had received in each parish he passed through. One unnamed parish, where he was whipped as a vagrant, received nothing at all! This part of the story, at least, is untrue because every parish in Surrey was rewarded in his will.

Over the centuries Surrey's inhabitants have benefited from a great variety of charities, some of distinctly unusual character – none more so than that established by the will of John How of Guildford, who died in 1674. He left £400 which was to be invested to provide an annual prize in a contest which became known as 'Dicing for the Maid's Money'. Two contestants were chosen from female servants of good character who had resided in the ancient borough of Guildford for at least two years. The winner was to be decided by the throw of a dice. The loser, however, gained consolation from the fact that she could try again for the next two years. More recently, the loser has also received the unclaimed money left by John Parsons in his will of 1702 for the benefit of Guildford apprentices. Despite the occasional difficulty in finding suitable contestants these days, John How's charity still continues. In 1994 the winner threw a double five and won £50. Meanwhile, the loser with a paltry four got £52 from the proceeds of John Parsons' charity!

Reigate Priory, seen here in an 18th century engraving, was the home of Lord Howard of Effingham, High Admiral of the English fleet which defeated the Spanish Armada.

A few elderly paupers might have been lucky enough to find accommodation in one of a number of almshouses or hospitals established in Surrey during Tudor or Jacobean times. The most important of these from the reign of Elizabeth I was Whitgift's Hospital at Croydon. The red brick gabled almshouse, which still stands today amidst the modern roar of suburban Croydon, was endowed by John Whitgift, Archbishop of Canterbury, and built between 1596 and 1599. It was to be '. . . an hospitall and abiding place for the finding, sustentation and relief of certain maymed poore, needy or impotent people to have continuance for ever . . .' The statutes of Whitgift's Hospital limited the number of inmates to between 30 and 40 – '. . . of which number, one shall teach a common school in Croydon in the schoole house there by me builded.' Thus the founding of the hospital was also the origin of Whitgift Grammar School.

The origins of the grammar school at Guildford go back to the will of Robert Beckingham who died in 1512. Beckingham left land to finance the establishment of a free school in the town. Also at Guildford, another Archbishop of Canterbury, George Abbot, founded a hospital similar to Whitgift's during the reign of James I. Abbot's Hospital, as it became known, will be mentioned in more detail later.

Charity alone proved insufficient to solve the problems caused by the increasing number of poor and destitute in Tudor England. Eventually, the first Poor Laws were passed. They ensured that all who could afford it were legally obliged to contribute to the welfare of the genuinely needy.

In 1588 all the people of England, regardless of their wealth or status, were under threat. With news of the approach of the Spanish Armada, Surrey was called upon to supply 1,000 troops to help guard against any invasion approaching London up the Thames estuary. A further 500 were sent to London itself. In July 1588, with the Armada in sight in the Channel, all able bodied men were called to arms for the protection of the realm. The motley collection of weapons available to the 5,000 or so Surrey men involved were nowhere near the quality of those confiscated from Thomas Cawarden back in 1554, but they mustered all the same at camps at Dorking, Reigate, Croydon and Godstone. There they waited for the signal from beacons which would be set ablaze on prominences such as Leith Hill, Betchworth Clump and Hindhead when the first of the enemy had landed. They readied themselves as best they could for the onslaught from those well-armed foreign troops, who at that very moment were feeling seasick on the foaming waters of the English Channel.

Although the charismatic figure of Francis Drake is the first to spring to mind when recalling one of England's proudest moments, it was

Lord Charles Howard of Effingham, who commanded the English fleet at the defeat of the Armada in 1588.

Lord Charles Howard of Effingham as Lord High Admiral, who gave the lead to the English sailors. As the Armada approached, Lord Howard conducted operations from on board his flagship, *The Ark Royal.* His brilliance as a commander, coupled with the fearless persistence of his sailors, plus a little help from England's most familiar friend, bad weather, saw off the invaders and showed Europe that England was once more a force to be reckoned with. The Armada beacons were never fired.

Lord Charles Howard of Effingham, eldest son of Lord William Howard, had inherited the family estates centred on Reigate Priory in 1581. As a child he had been educated mainly at Reigate by John Foxe, the author of the famous *Book of Martyrs*. In 1553, when Howard was 17, Foxe, being a Protestant, fled abroad to escape the attentions of Queen Mary. The following year Howard began his career as a soldier when he fought in France, but it was not long before he was serving in the navy, which had been established by Henry VIII. He was popular at court under Mary and managed to maintain his position when Elizabeth became queen in 1558. The following year she sent him as a special ambassador to France. In 1573 he was made a Knight of the Garter and in 1584 Lord High Admiral, an appointment he retained until 1619. He was created Earl of Nottingham in 1596 in recognition of his skills when the English fleet captured Cadiz and destroyed the Spanish fleet sheltering there. Lord Howard

Sir Walter Raleigh, whose head is buried in West Horsley church.

died, aged 88, in 1624, recognised by all as one of the greatest men of his time, and was buried in the family vault in Reigate parish church.

Amongst the heroes of 1588 there was also, of course, Sir Walter Raleigh. His brilliant exploits as a sailor and navigator had made him a favourite of Elizabeth and in 1585 he had been knighted. However, in 1592 he fell from grace for a while as a result of his secret marriage to one of the queen's maids-of-honour. Both Sir Walter and his bride were put in the Tower for a time. This was the first of three visits to the dreaded prison for Sir Walter. Under James I he was distinctly unpopular at court and spent twelve years in the place. He was then released, only to be returned shortly afterwards for a final, fatal visit, which ended when he was beheaded. His widow had the head embalmed and kept it with her until she died in 1647. The head was then passed to Sir Walter's son, Carew Raleigh, who lived at West Horsley Place. Three of Carew's children, including his eldest son, Walter also (like his grandfather Sir Walter), died in 1660 and were buried under the floor in St Mary's church in West Horsley. It was probably at this time that Carew decided to pop his father's head into the family burial place as

Richmond Palace where Elizabeth I died on 24th March 1603.

well and there it lies to this day. The body was interred in St Margaret's, Westminster, but it is said to walk the corridors of West Horsley Place searching for his head – a gruesome finale for one of the heroes of 1588.

In her last weeks Elizabeth returned once more to Surrey, the county which held many happy memories for her. Her time seemed past, for those most dear to her were already dead. It was the loss of her great confidant and advisor, William Cecil, Lord Burghley, in 1598, which particularly laid her low. And then there was her undoubted guilt concerning the execution of the Earl of Essex, a man she surely loved. The mere mention of his name now brought her near to tears. At Richmond Palace she sat long hours in silence, refusing to rest 'because she had a persuasion that if she once lay down she would never rise.' Her council begged her to name her successor and she is said to have finally replied, 'I will that a king succeed me, and who but my kinsman the King of Scots.' Rest finally came to the great queen at Richmond on 24th March 1603.

10

ARCHBISHOPS AND THE CIVIL WAR

It is hard to believe that Croydon, where tower blocks and traffic laden roads now dominate, was once the chosen site for the Archbishop of Canterbury's summer palace. But here, where the clear, sparkling waters of the river Wandle bubbled out of the ground at the foot of the chalk downs and the air was clean and pure, was the ideal spot. And it was within easy reach of London. Croydon had belonged to the Archbishops since the Conquest but it was probably during the 12th century that it became a favourite residence. Despite the icy blasts of 1960s architects, who swept most of ancient Croydon away, much of the palace has survived.

The palace consists of two courtyards enclosed by an irregular group of buildings, some with a second floor. The great hall, situated on the ground floor, measures 56 ft by 38 ft and has some fine timber-framing. It was originally built by Archbishop Courtney in the late 14th century, but most of what survives today is the work of Archbishop Stafford in the mid-15th century. To the west of the hall, a 17th century staircase leads to the great parlour, also known as Arundel's Hall as it was built by Archbishop Arundel in the early 15th century. Other features from the same century include the brick-built chapel and the library. There is also a fine 16th century long gallery, timber-framed with later brick facing. The palace is now a school.

As far as Surrey is concerned, Croydon Palace's most famous resident was George Abbot, who was Archbishop of Canterbury between 1611 and 1633. Abbot was born at Guildford in 1562. His father, Maurice, was a staunchly Protestant clothworker of limited means, who had been persecuted during the reign of Queen Mary. The father's views formed the basis of the son's Christian outlook and right from his birth great things were expected of George. It is claimed that his mother had a dream foretelling fortune and fame for the child she was carrying. This story was retold over a hundred years later by John Aubrey, whose *Natural History and Antiquities of the County of Surrey*, written mainly in the late 1670s, was published in five volumes in 1718/19:

Croydon Palace was once the favourite summer residence of the Archbishops of Canterbury. (Surrey Archaeological Society)

'... his Mother, when she was with Child of him, dream't, that if she could eat a Jack or Pike, her Son in her Womb would be a great Man, upon this she was indefatigable to satisfy her Longing, as well as her Dream: She first enquir'd out for this Fish; but accidently taking up some of the River Water (that runs close by the House) in a Pail, she took up the much desir'd Banquet, dress'd it, and devour'd it almost all: This odd Affair made no small Noise in the Neighbourhood, and the Curiosity of it made several People of Quality offer themselves to be Sponsors at the Baptismal Fount when she was deliver'd ...'

George Abbot's birthplace was adjacent to the Town Bridge in Guildford, opposite St Nicolas' parish church. His mother's dream can probably be put down to that desire for unusual foods often experienced by pregnant women! The Abbot home eventually became a pub under the sign of the Three Mariners and survived until 1864, when it was demolished. The sponsors mentioned by John Aubrey safely saw George through his education at Guildford Grammar School and then at Oxford University. He entered the church and in 1600 became Vice-Chancellor of his university. He was a very gifted scholar in classical languages and was responsible for translating into English parts of James I's new 'Authorised Version' of the Bible. It is this classic translation which is still widely used throughout the English Church today. Thus George

84

Abbot's fame as foretold at his birth seemed destined to be in the field of scholarship. Therefore, it was something of a surprise when the king nominated him as Archbishop of Canterbury in 1611.

Tensions within the Church of England were beginning to come to a head during the reign of James I. On the one hand, there were those with puritan beliefs, who hated anything in the Church and its services which they thought of as 'popish', and, on the other, there were those who at the extreme held views akin to the Catholics. Abbot, with his strong Protestant ideals, was not perhaps the best of choices as archbishop. A late-19th century biographer pinpointed the problem when he wrote that Abbot was '... "stiffly principled" in puritan doctrines, and his

George Abbot, Archbishop of Canterbury 1611–1633, who was born in Guildford in 1562.

views, cast in a dangerously narrow mould, took from his habitually gloomy and morose temperament a fanatical colouring.' What was really wanted was an archbishop with the diplomatic skills to hold the rival factions within the Church together. George Abbot did not possess such skills. The leader of the 'High Church' faction or 'Arminians' as they were known, was William Laud, a man whom Abbot hated. Their clashes over many years highlighted the grave problems brewing within the Church. Thus were sown some of the seeds of the Civil War, which was to tear the country apart later in the century.

Whatever his failings as an archbishop, George Abbot often remembered the town of his birth and he returned the generosity which the inhabitants of Guildford had shown to him in his early days. In 1619 the building of his 'Hospital of the Blessed Trinity' began at the top of Guildford's High Street. It was to be an almshouse for twelve 'Brothers' and eight 'Sisters', who were single elderly Guildfordians – a place of peace and comfort in the last years of their lives. Rooms for the residents were built round a courtyard, with a chapel and common rooms. An impressive gatehouse with domed octagonal towers faced out to the street as it does to this day. With extra accommodation provided recently by building over part of the garden at the rear, 'Abbot's Hospital', as it is more popularly known, still provides for the elderly of the town.

In 1621 Abbot was involved in an accident whilst hunting in Hampshire, when a gamekeeper was killed by an arrow accidentally fired from the Archbishop's cross-bow. For a man of Abbot's temperament this incident proved to be a tragic blow and, although King James forgave him, it provided opponents like William Laud with further means to bring the Archbishop down. It was now Laud who held the real power in the Church and the unfortunate George Abbot, whilst remaining Archbishop of Canterbury, went into virtual retirement. When James I died in 1625 Abbot's main support had gone and, although he emerged to crown Charles I, it was Laud who had the ear of the new king. George Abbot lingered on until 1633, when his death gave Laud the mitre he had coveted so long.

Abbot was buried in the town of his birth, where his splendid tomb in Holy Trinity church has survived the rebuilding of the church itself in the 1750s. Abbot was a man of compassion and charity, especially to the people of his home town, and indeed a 'great man'. His tomb has pillars supported on books beautifully carved in alabaster, showing to all where he truly found the greatness his mother's dream foretold.

Laud set about searching out and eradicating those puritan elements in the Church which he despised so much. As a result, a split in the Church was inevitable and, for opposite reasons, he was no more the right man for the job than George Abbot had been. Charles I was not a Romanist but it was natural that those of that ilk would side with their monarch, whilst Parliament came to represent the voice of the strongly Protestant. Charles believed in the absolute power of the monarchy as a god given right and attempted to rule without Parliament. But without Parliament's right to grant direct general taxation he had to find other, increasingly unpopular, means of raising money, to fill his exchequer. In Surrey, as in many other counties, he attempted to reimpose the laws of the forest, as all fines and fees from the forest courts went directly to him. The king had his way in this respect but great was his loss of support throughout the county. His arbitrary enclosure of land adjacent to Richmond Palace as a hunting ground in 1636, whilst being of outstanding benefit to succeeding generations, caused a great deal of anger and dissatisfaction at the time.

Furthermore, there was the imposition of 'Ship Money', ostensibly to pay for the navy. It was assessed on property and collected by the king's shire representative, the county sheriff, and paid directly into the king's exchequer. There is no reason to believe that, although as a tax it was unconstitutional, each town's contribution was not fairly calculated.

Abbot's Hospital at Guildford, built in 1619, from a sketch by Duncan Moul in 1902

Therefore, the Ship Money assessment of 1636 is of great interest for the evidence it gives of the comparative prosperity of Surrey's towns at the time. For example, Farnham was assessed at £94, Godalming at £90 and Kingston at £88, but Guildford, where the cloth industry had recently collapsed, raised a mere £53. Dorking and Reigate were little better off than the county town at £58 and £60 respectively. It was an extremely unpopular tax, which Sir Nicholas Stoughton, the sheriff in 1637, had a great deal of trouble collecting. But Stoughton, a Puritan and, as H.E. Malden wrote, '. . . friend to the Dutch, against whose naval insolences ship money was needed, member for Guildford in . . . Parliament and active opponent of the king, was not very anxious that ship money should be collected if he could get out of it decently.' Eventually, despite these various schemes to squeeze money from his subjects, Charles was forced to recall Parliament in 1640.

The return of Parliament brought about an upsurge of persecution, not only of Roman Catholics but also against any members of the Anglican clergy thought to have papist tendencies. It was a time to

87

settle old scores and many a minister was thrown out on the strength of dubious evidence. The unfortunate parson of Compton, Myrth Waferer, whose life now ceased to live up to his name, became only the second incumbent in England to be ejected as a result of this latest inquisition. In 1643 Nicholas Andrewes, Vicar of Godalming, was also ejected when four members of his flock were prepared to accuse him of a variety of misdemeanours. They claimed that he was a 'haunter and frequenter of tiplings in Innes and Tavernes' and that he had numerous crucifixes and 'Romish' pictures hanging in his vicarage. Andrewes was further accused, in company with his already ejected colleague from nearby Compton, that they had gone together to Southampton to eat fish and had toasted the health of the Pope, calling him 'that honest old man'. Andrewes was imprisoned and died as a result of the ill-treatment he received there.

By the time of Andrewes' death the disagreements between Parliament and King Charles had reached the point of open conflict. Even before Charles had raised his standard at Nottingham in August 1642, thus declaring his intention to fight Parliament, Peter Quennell of Lythe Hill, Haslemere, had gathered a small force in support of the king. Quennell was apparently a captain in the local militia but he was also an iron-master at one of the local ironworks at Imbhams, where he 'made gunns and shotte for his Majestie's stores'. He must have realised the importance of holding such facilities for the king and raised a force of 74 men, who came mainly from the tithings of the Godalming Hundred, to defend the ironworks and its stores. But the poorly armed force was quickly overpowered by the county authorities who, even at this early stage, were firmly on the Parliamentary side. There were rumours of a Royalist plot to seize Kingston but this also came to nothing. Kingston was important for the strategic value of its bridge over the Thames and for the fact that it also housed the county's magazine of guns and ammunition. The town was hurriedly occupied for Parliament by a force under Sir Richard Onslow.

Most of the fighting in Surrey during the Civil War centred around the Bishop of Winchester's castle at Farnham. In October 1642 Parliament appointed George Wither, who was a famous poet in his time, as governor of the castle. Following the first major battle of the war at Edgehill on 23rd October 1642, Royalist forces swept down on Surrey from the north-west and took the castle at Farnham without a fight. The small number of poorly armed defenders had already made good their escape before the king's forces arrived. Sir John Denham of Egham, the newly appointed High Sheriff was now the Royalist governor.

By 9th November Prince Rupert's Royalist cavalry had crossed the Thames and were encamped at Oatlands, but the following day they withdrew to Egham and then recrossed the river by way of Staines Bridge. Later, following a confrontation with the enemy at Turnham Green in Middlesex, King Charles briefly occupied Kingston and for a short time was also at Oatlands.

Farnham was of immense strategic value to both sides in the conflict. From the Royalist point of view it guarded important roads, which could lead them from their strongholds in the west, not only to London but also across south Surrey and Sussex. From there they could link up with the strong band of their supporters in Kent. Therefore, it was imperative for the Parliamentary cause that Farnham Castle be retaken.

A Parliamentary force led by Sir William Waller was at the gates of Farnham Castle a fortnight after Wither's evacuation. Sir John Denham had little more success than Wither in defending the place. On 26th November Waller blew up the gates and, after a brief fight, in which there were casualties on both sides, the Royalists surrendered. On 29th December Waller ordered the blowing up of the north-eastern wall of the shell-keep of the castle. Despite the damage, Waller continued to use the castle as a base for the crucial conflicts in the area during the following two years. These were centred around Winchester and Basing House, near Basingstoke, in adjacent Hampshire, and also in Sussex, where Arundel Castle and Chichester, having been lost to the Royalists in 1643, were recaptured during the early days of 1644.

Two events at Farnham stand out from the many occurring in the area during these troubled times. In the autumn of 1643 Waller was given a new commission to form the Southern Association Army, mainly made up of men drawn from Surrey, Hampshire, Sussex and Kent. At the time, to the west of Farnham, a Royalist army led by Sir Ralph Hopton was gathering strength. Therefore, Waller's new army was ordered to muster at Farnham and by the end of October the town was full to bursting with over 7,000 troops. They were billeted in Farnham and the surrounding villages as far east as Godalming.

On 1st November 1643 the Southern Association Army mustered in Farnham Park, where they were reviewed by Sir William Waller. Here, no doubt, they received a pep talk from their commander and also registered for the purposes of receiving pay. Most importantly, they would also have received training in how to recognise the standards and colours of the various units which made up the army – a most crucial matter if friend were to be separated from foe during battlefield charges and close hand-to-hand fighting. At the review, a soldier described as a 'clerk' from Waller's own regiment of foot was court-martialled. He may well have been caught with his hand in the pay-chest, but, for whatever reason, he was found guilty before the assembled army and sentenced to death. The execution took place in Farnham Park the following day, when the unfortunate man was hanged from a tree.

At dawn on 27th November Hopton's Royalist army of 8,000 or so troops appeared through the mist '. . . upon a hill two miles from Farnham . . . between Crundle and Farnham'. On receiving news of the enemy's approach, those Parliamentary troops billeted in town formed up in Farnham Park with 'the ordnance placed about a mile and a half from their [Royalist] body of horse'. Another eye-witness described the Royalists as being '. . . in a great body upon a hill, in the heath above the Parke, about a mile from us'. Looking down on Farnham, Sir Ralph Hopton later wrote that he '. . . drew out all his horse and foote, . . . presented himself in battell upon the nearest part of the heath towards Farnham'.

Hopton sent forward about 1,000 musketeers and some cavalry into the park. It seems that the opposing forces then faced each other in stalemate. Waller remained in a defensive position on the east side of the castle, with some of his cavalry and dragoons hidden from the Royalists behind a small hill. He had had insufficient warning to bring in all his troops billeted in outlying areas and was thus heavily outnumbered. However, he had the advantage that the forward troops of the enemy were well within range of his cannon. The stalemate continued throughout the day – Hopton not daring to expose his main force to the Parliamentary guns and Waller not wishing to move his smaller force from its defensive position. Eventually, three of Waller's guns boomed out and the Royalist's advance party drew back, leaving a number of casualties. Waller followed up with some of his cavalry and there followed a series of bloody skirmishes. Running fights continued into the night as Hopton's forces withdrew. This serious incident might have developed into one of the major battles of the Civil War. In the event, this battle took place at Cheriton, near Alresford in Hampshire, on 29th March 1644, when Hopton's army was destroyed.

By 1648 all organised Royalist resistance had collapsed and King Charles was a prisoner in the Isle of Wight. But there was festering dissatisfaction amongst the ordinary folk of England, tired of war and, in particular, of the crippling imposition of billeted troops and the levies to pay the soldiers' wages. The army was far from popular and open revolt lay just beneath the surface. In May, following a meeting of protestors at Dorking attended by a large number of Surrey inhabitants, matters came to a head. After gathering further support for their petition from throughout the county, a large group of Surrey men marched on Westminster. They, 'being all true Protestants', prayed 'that the king, their only lawful sovereign, might be restored to his due honour, and

The ruins of Farnham Castle in about 1850. The castle was the main centre of activity in Surrey during the Civil War.

come to the parliament for a personal treaty; that unnatural wars may be prevented from beginning again; that the ordinances against the unsupportable burthen of free-quarter for the soldiers may be executed and the army disbanded, their pay being discharged.'

Unfortunately, those 'unnatural wars' did begin again for, even as the petition was being presented to Parliament, 'a tumult took place in the passages to the House, and in Westminster Hall; and on the soldiers on guard being reinforced to suppress it, a few of the petitioners were seized and committed to prison, and others dispersed and fled; some lives having been lost on both sides.' Open insurrection now began in Kent, Essex and other counties. In Surrey a small Royalist army of about five or six hundred troops, led by the weak and indecisive Earl of Holland, accompanied by the Duke of Buckingham and his brother, Lord Francis Villiers, raised its standard at Kingston.

As a precaution, the order went out for the destruction of castles such as Farnham and Reigate. The authorities were mindful, no doubt, of the earlier problems there had been, when Royalists had succeeded in holding out for long periods of time behind fortifications like those at Basing House in Hampshire. The keep at Farnham, already damaged in 1642, was apparently blown up, although it appears to have survived into the 18th century in remarkably good condition.

Holland's force gathered on Banstead Downs on the pretext of attending a horse race, but Parliament already had intelligence of these plans and dispatched a force under Major Audeley. He arrived too late to intercept the Royalists at Banstead for they had already moved on to Reigate. Here Audeley's force attacked a guard which Holland had stationed on Red Hill and successfully drove them off. But when Holland's main force appeared, Audeley held back for reinforcements, whereupon, instead of attacking, the Royalists turned round and marched to Dorking. The following morning Holland had his troops back in Reigate again, where they arrived just in time to confront the troops led by Colonel Livesey sent to augment Major Audeley's force. Indecision turned to ignoble flight as the Royalists now turned towards Ewell, hotly pursued by Livesey's force. Skirmishes took place at Ewell and in Nonsuch Park, where Livesey took several prisoners. Finally, on a hill at Surbiton, the Royalists turned and stood their ground but, as Audeley reported afterwards, Holland's men 'after a gallant defence, and as sharp a charge as ever I saw in these unhappy wars, were routed'. However, many of the Royalist forces managed to escape to Kingston where, under cover of darkness, they dispersed.

Amongst those who died at the 'Battle of Surbiton Common' was the youthful Lord Francis Villiers, whose heroic end was later described by John Aubrey, '. . . in the Lane between Kyngston and Sathbyton Common, was slain the beautiful Francis Viliers, at an Elm in the Hedge of the East Side of the Lane, where, his Horse being killed under him, he turned his back to the Elm, and fought most valiantly with half a dozen'. Unfortunately for Lord Francis, one of the Roundheads most unsportingly climbed through the hedge further down the lane and crept up behind him and 'coming on the other Side of the Hedge, push'd off his Helmet, and killed him.' Lord Francis Villiers had perished in the last battle to be fought in Surrey.

The Earl of Holland was captured shortly after this debacle and sentenced to suffer the same fate as his king. On 19th December 1648 King Charles crossed from the Isle of Wight under heavy guard en route to his trial and execution. On the night of 20th December he was lodged in the house of Henry Vernon in West Street, Farnham. Vernon House has survived to this day and is now part of the Farnham Public Library. Many local people crowded into the room where Charles took his supper, just for the chance to look at him, despite the threatening presence of his guards. When he departed for Bagshot the following morning, Charles presented the Vernons with a morning cap as a keepsake. Five weeks later he was dead.

TIMES OF PEACE

In the late 1670s John Aubrey wrote of a village once known as Ebbesham, 'It is celebrated for the Medicated Spring there; which was first discovered about 1639 or 1640, by some Labourers accidently drinking there. In the year 1654, or 1655, I was there, and drank of them. I experimented it only by Evaporation, and it yielded (from about a Gallon) a Sediment of flakey Stuff, of the Colour of Bay-Salt, in loose Flakes, as much as fill'd a Tobacco-Box . . . It purgeth very well'. The name of Ebbesham became corrupted to Epsom and what Aubrey was writing about was, of course, the famous source of Epsom salts.

With the restoration of King Charles II, Epsom developed into a famous spa, where all those of fashion journeyed to take the waters, which Aubrey described as tasting bitter '. . . together with a maukish Saltiness'. At Epsom facilities for visitors were developed which were far superior at the time to those to be found at the rival spas of Tunbridge Wells and Bath. There were fine inns and places of entertainment, assembly rooms, bowling greens and cock pits. Epsom could also claim the invigorating properties of its clean air, with the added attraction of horse racing on the chalk downs to the south.

Samuel Pepys came to Epsom in July 1663 and found the place so crowded that he had to go as far as Ashtead to find some lodgings. When he went to the well the following day he found 'a great store of citizens there though some of better quality'. Pepys drank two pots of the water, noting the instant effect and 'how everybody turns up his tail . . . in a bush'. He returned exactly four years later with his wife and her friend and wrote in his diary, 'A very fine day, and so towards Epsum, talking all the way pleasantly . . . The country very fine, only the way very dusty. We got to Epsum by eight o'clock, to the well; where much company, and there we 'light, and I drank the water: they did not . . . I did drink four pints, and had some very good stools by it.' Epsom was full of people he knew – 'Here I met with divers of our town', and at dinner in the King's Head he noted that '. . . my Lord Backhurst and Nelly [Gwynn] are lodged at the next house, and Sir Charles Sidley.'

The original discovery of the water had been made on Epsom Common to the south-west of what was then just a village, but the supply of water from it often proved insufficient to meet demand. Eventually, during the 1690s, a second source was discovered, conveniently situated adjacent to the town. This new well was promoted by an entrepreneurial apothecary named Livingstone. He soon began to develop the area around the new well by building gaming rooms, a dance hall, shops and a bowling green. Livingstone understood the power of advertising, and in 1707 the following appeared in the *Daily Courant*:

'The new Wells at Epsom, with variety of Rafling-Shops will be open'd on Easter Monday next. There are Shops now to be let at the said Wells for a Bookseller, Pictures, Haberdasher of Hats, Shoomaker, Fishmonger and Butcher, with Conveniences for several other Trades. It is design'd that a very good Consort of Musick shall attend and play there Morning and Evening during the Season and nothing will be demanded for the Waters drank there.'

'Rafling-Shops' were the gaming rooms, especially for games with dice. The business acumen of Mr Livingstone is obvious from this advertisement – he aimed to attract customers by allowing them to take the waters free, but he made his money from the shops' rents and the gaming rooms. When Celia Fiennes travelled to Epsom in the late 1690s she visited the original well and described the wellhouse as '. . . so dark and unpleasant, more like a dungeon that I would not chuse to drinke in there'. She came again in about 1712 and found arrangements considerably improved, '. . . and now the Wells are built about and a large light roome to walk in brick'd, and a pump put on the Well, a coffee house and two roomes for gameing, and shops for sweetmeates and fruite'.

Livingstone died in 1727 and his death marked the beginning of the rapid decline of the Epsom wells. Facilities at Bath and Tunbridge Wells were now better than at Epsom and there was further competition from a number of new spas and wells. Also the volume of water available from the Epsom wells was limited. As Celia Fiennes noted, 'its not a quick spring and very often is dranke drye, and to make up the defficiency the people do often carry water from common wells to fill this in a morning (this they have been found out in) which makes the water weake and of little opperation unless you can have it first from the well before they can have put in any other'. Chemists had also been eagerly at work analysing the chemical content of Epsom water. Magnesium sulphate or 'Epsom Salts' was now readily manufactured and sold at any apothecary's shop.

Samuel Pepys dined at the King's Head, Epsom, when visiting the famous wells in 1667. This photograph dates from 1910 but the building has since been demolished.

Samuel Pepys recorded not just trips to Epsom in his famous diary. In his official capacity as Secretary to the Admiralty, he often travelled along the road to Portsmouth, staying at several of Surrey's famous inns which had sprung up along the route. For all the towns and villages on this famous road, catering for the thirst and hunger of its weary travellers was a lucrative source of income. Thus there were important inns in Kingston, at Esher, Ripley, Guildford and Godalming. The last two towns were situated conveniently near the halfway point of the journey and competition for customers between them was often fierce.

In early August 1668 Pepys made a journey from London to Petersfield, in Hampshire, for a meeting with Admiral Sir Thomas Allen, John Tippetts, Commissioner of the Navy, and Colonel Fitzgerald. The course and condition of the road was such that a guide was needed for some parts of the journey and 'around Cobham' his coach got lost for 'three or four mile'. At Guildford his party, which included his wife and her maid, dined and there Pepys 'shewed them the hospitall there of Bishop Abbot's, and his tomb in the church, which, and the rest of the tombs there, are kept mighty clean and neat, with curtains before them.' The most difficult and potentially dangerous part of the journey was the

95

long grind from Thursley and up over Hind Common above the Devil's Punchbowl. Here highwaymen and footpads often took advantage of this isolated spot and there is a hint of fear in Pepys' diary when he says, '. . . got to Lippock, late over Hindhead, having an old man, a guide, in the coach with us; but got thither with great fear of being out of our way, it being ten at night.'

On the return journey from his meeting, Pepys came to Guildford for the night, where he found '. . . the Red Lyon so full of people, and a wedding, that the master of the house did get us a lodging over the way, at a private house, his landlord's, mighty neat and fine; and there supped and talked with the landlord and his wife; and so to bed with great content'. The Red Lion Inn in the High Street was one of the town's famous inns, which also included the White Hart, the White Lion and the Angel. Of these, only the Angel survives to this day, although the much vandalised building which was once the Red Lion still stands on the corner of Market Street.

In 1698 the King's Arms at Godalming accommodated its most famous visitors – Tsar Peter the Great of Russia and his entourage, who were returning from Portsmouth where they had been to watch ships of the English navy on manoeuvres. Landlord James Moon soon came to regret the Russians' choice of lodgings, as they proceeded to consume vast quantities of food and drink with little obvious sign of payment. A contemporary list of the contents of the Russians' gastronomic orgy is preserved in the Bodleian Library at Oxford. The Russians ate at breakfast half a sheep, ten pullets, twelve chickens, seven dozen eggs, washed down with three quarts of brandy and six quarts of mulled wine. At dinner they are said to have eaten five ribs of beef, one sheep, three quarters of lamb, one shoulder of boiled veal, eight pullets, eight rabbits and drunk thirty bottles of sack and twelve bottles of claret. To the relief of all in Godalming, they soon departed to the London house of John Evelyn, a diarist as famous as Pepys, at Deptford, where they stayed three months. Evelyn recorded that their riotous behaviour at Deptford caused £150 worth of damage to the house and its garden. But he left any personal comments about them to his bailiff, who described them succinctly as 'right nasty'.

John Evelyn was a man of remarkable talents, who was born at Wotton near Dorking in 1620. His grandfather had made the family fortune by obtaining the monopoly for the manufacture of gunpowder in 1589. John Evelyn's vast diary is in part a memoir, but he started compiling it when he was eight. It covers a long period when England was transformed from a comparatively minor but enterprising nation into a major power on the verge of building a great empire. It was thinking

The King's Arms, Godalming, where Tsar Peter the Great stayed in 1698. This view shows the famous hostelry in about 1890.

men like Evelyn who made a major contribution to this change, especially in the arts.

John Evelyn's interests were as catholic as his Christianity was not and throughout his life he held to a pious Protestantism. It is probably not surprising, therefore, that his diary lacks the 'earthiness' of Samuel Pepys. Whilst Pepys recorded the everyday incidents of life with wit and humanity, Evelyn was apt to go home and criticize. At Charles II's court there was a great deal of gambling, which was one of the king's favourite pastimes. Pepys carefully observed the effects on his fellow man of the turn of the dice, commenting, 'And mighty glad I am that I did see it . . . which did give me another pretty observation of a man'. Meanwhile, a shocked Evelyn wrote of seeing '. . . deepe and prodigious gaming . . . vast heaps of Gold squandered away in a vaine and profuse manner. This I looked on as an horrid vice, and unsuitable

The Spread Eagle, Epsom, was originally one of the town's famous inns during the heyday of the wells. The building has now been converted into a shopping precinct.

to a Christian Court.' Evelyn and Pepys were well acquainted with each other and sometimes dined together – the most unusual occasion being in the Tower of London in 1679, where Pepys had been temporarily incarcerated for alleged 'misdemeanours in the Admiralty'.

Much of Evelyn's early life was divided between Wotton and Lewes in Sussex, where he was educated. He then went up to Oxford University and in 1641 he made a tour of Holland and the Spanish Netherlands to broaden his education. During the Civil War, as a supporter of the king, he saw the wisdom of further foreign travel during the worst times, thereby keeping out of trouble and preserving the family's extensive estates in Surrey. In this diary he recorded many details of what he saw on his journeys in Holland, France, Italy and Switzerland. Already he was particularly interested in architecture and gardens, especially trees and landscaping.

In Paris he visited the Tuileries and Fontainebleau and became a friend of Sir Richard Browne, the royal ambassador, and his circle of Royalist exiles. He made careful note of the orchards of Normandy and the chateau at Chambord in the Loire valley, which he was 'desirous of seeing' because of the 'extravagance of the designe, especially the Stayre-Case mention'd by the Architect Palladio'. In Italy he visited the famous tower at Pisa, commenting that '. . . the beholder would expect every moment when it should fall; being built exceedingly declining by a rare adresse of the imortal Architect: . . . how it is supported from immediately falling would puzzle a good Geometrician.' In Rome he was much taken by the 'sweete and delicious' Tivoli Gardens. At Geneva Evelyn went down with smallpox and was kept '. . . in bed for 16 daies, tended by a vigilant Swisse Matron whose monstrous throat, when I sometimes awake'd . . . would affright me.' Fortunately, he recovered and returned to Paris, where he married Sir Richard Browne's daughter, Mary.

Evelyn returned to England in October 1647, leaving his young wife in France. She finally came to England to join her husband in 1652. Evelyn maintained secret contact with the exiles in France via letters addressed to Mr Peters, an alias for his father-in-law, using a secret code and signing the letters 'Aphanos'. Evelyn was back in France in 1649, taking the distressing details of Charles I's death to the exiled Queen Henrietta. He finally returned to England in early 1652 and was followed later in the year by his wife. During the years of the Commonwealth, he managed to maintain a low profile, whilst keeping in touch with the English court in France.

With the restoration of Charles II, it was not surprising that Evelyn should find himself a regular visitor to court, where his discussions with the king ranged over such diverse subjects as ships' varnish and perpetual motion. It is said that Evelyn was offered a knighthood on three occasions but refused it each time. He now lived primarily at Sayes Court in Deptford, the house which was to suffer later at the hands of Tsar Peter and his friends. However, he made regular visits to Wotton, the home of his eldest brother, George, and to his brother Richard at Woodcote near Epsom.

In October 1664, during the war with the Dutch, Evelyn was appointed a Commissioner for the Wounded and Prisoners of War. When the plague struck London in the summer of 1665, his work as Commissioner kept him some of the time in London and thus in grave danger. On 28th August he recorded, 'The Contagion growing now all about us, I sent my Wife and whole family (two or three of my necessary servants excepted) to Wotton to my Brothers, being resolved to stay at my house my selfe, and to look after my Charge, trusting in providence and goodnesse of God.' Providence and God succeeded, for Evelyn survived whilst thousands around him perished. There was a danger that the disease would be carried down the main routes out of London and thus into Surrey. In the 1640s there had been several serious outbreaks of the plague in Surrey towns, when Parliamentary troops were billeted throughout much of the county. But in 1665 the disease confined its worst to the capital and, in the isolation of Wotton, Evelyn's family were also spared.

In January 1661, John Evelyn had been made a Fellow of the new

John Evelyn (1620–1706), the famous diarist, who is buried in Wotton church.

'Philosophic Society', later to become the Royal Society. He had already written or translated a number of works, but in 1664 the book which brought greatest recognition in his lifetime, *Sylva, or a Discourse of Forest Trees in His Majestie's Dominions*, was published. Evelyn was putting down on paper much of what he had practised at Wotton, influenced by what he had seen during his Continental tour, particularly in Italy. The entry in his diary for 22nd February 1652 records a visit with George to Wotton 'to give him what directions I was able about his Garden, which he was now desirous to put into some forme: but for which he was to remove a mountaine'.

The result of this 'mountain moving' was an artificial tree-covered terraced hill above a mock Roman temple, a fountain supplied by an aqueduct from the nearby river Tillingbourne and a long avenue of chestnut trees. Later generations of the Evelyn family have altered the house beyond John Evelyn's recognition but his garden remains relatively intact. Also surviving is the garden the Evelyns designed at Albury Park, a few miles down the Tillingbourne valley from Wotton. Here a series of terraces were constructed along the side of a hill, with a large cavern in imitation of a Roman bath beneath the main terrace. A tunnel was also dug right through the hill, emerging in front of a fountain fed by an elaborate watercourse and conduit, which brought water round the side of the hill from a source at the foot of the chalk downs. This element of the Evelyns' garden has recently been restored.

During the 19th century the Evelyn family had a penchant for exotic pets, keeping terrapins at Wotton in a grandly built 'tortoise house' with an Ionic portico. Their famous ancestor, John Evelyn, had also shown a great interest in unusual animals, carefully recording his observations in his diary. Whilst at Rotterdam in 1641, he had seen his first elephant and noted 'that I did never wonder at any thing more'. Over 200 years later, the family menagerie included kangaroos, but some of these escaped and for many years lived and bred in the wild around Leith Hill. John Evelyn would, no doubt, have been as impressed with them as he was when he saw that first elephant in Rotterdam.

12

THE GEORGIANS

In July 1685 the Duke of Monmouth was brought to Guildford on route to London and his execution. His untimely rising in the name of Protestantism against the Catholic James II had been badly misjudged and many of his followers now lay mutilated among the reeds and grasses of Sedgemoor. Many more were to receive the bloody judgement of Judge Jeffreys. Monmouth himself was discovered hiding in a Dorset ditch and came to Guildford a sad and broken man, shortly to meet the axeman on Tower Hill. At Guildford he was lodged overnight in a room high up in George Abbot's Hospital, where the modern visitor will still find the windows barred.

Following this small episode of excitement, the history of the county of Surrey follows a path of quiet development. It was still for most of its population an agricultural county but, here and there, various industrial enterprises also flourished. By the beginning of the 18th century the increasing prosperity of the country as a whole was reflected in the growth of its capital city. The rich merchants and traders of London now sought living space beyond the cramped streets of the city itself. It was natural that many of them should look to Surrey. Fine brick-built houses began to appear in areas then part of Surrey – from Camberwell to Clapham and along the banks of the Thames to Richmond and beyond. The very rich built even further out in the countryside, often on a very grand scale, and began to supplant the traditional country squire in many places. Surrey has many fine country houses of the period.

Tadworth Court, near Banstead, was built for Leonard Wessels, a London merchant of Dutch ancestry, sometime between 1694 and 1704. It was constructed in yellow brick with stone dressings and has an imposing Corinthian columned doorway with a carved stone lintel, approached by a flight of steps with stone balustrades. Frances Leaning, who wrote an excellent book about the house and its owners, published in 1928, described it as 'a simple, dignified and regular mass, a plain oblong in plan, without wings or gables, of lofty elevation, the angles of the slight projection in the front emphasized with bold quoins, the roof pierced by dormers springing therefrom above a widely-projecting cornice, the large-sashed windows carefully proportioned to the wall space, the chimney stacks in eight symmetrically-placed blocks.' Inside, a magnificent staircase with carved oak balustrades is the imposing centrepiece of the hall and leads up to a first floor gallery and a central corridor, which runs the full length of the house. The architect of this fine mansion is unknown, but Leaning has suggested that it may have been built to the same plans as those used for Ramsbury Manor in Wiltshire, a house designed by John Webb, a pupil of Inigo Jones. Today, Tadworth Court is the country branch of the Great Ormond Street Hospital for Sick Children.

The house at Westbrook on the outskirts of Godalming can never claim the excellence of architecture to be found at Tadworth Court. Its fame rests upon the activities of its most famous owner, James Oglethorpe, founder of the State of Georgia in the USA, named after King George II. The Oglethorpe connection with Westbrook began when James's father, Sir Theophilus Oglethorpe, bought the estate in 1688. James was born in London in 1696, the youngest of Sir Theophilus's three sons who lived beyond infancy. The oldest, Lewis, died as the result of a battle wound at The Hague in 1704 and the other son, Theophilus junior, relinquished all his titles to follow the Jacobite cause abroad. Theophilus senior died in 1702 and in 1718 James Oglethorpe became the squire of Westbrook. He was elected as one of two MPs for Haslemere in 1722. At Westminster, James soon acquired a reputation as a social reformer, particularly in respect of prisons. His interest in the plight of the country's prison inmates had first been aroused when a friend died of smallpox in a debtors' prison. In 1729 James Oglethorpe was appointed chairman of a committee which investigated the prison problem. The committee's report revealed a catalogue of bribery and cruelty and sowed the seeds of an idea in his mind – that the colonisation of lands in the new world could be a remedy for the worst evils of poverty and repression in the old.

The Gentlemen's Magazine reported on Monday, 30th October 1732: 'The *Ann* Galley, of above 200 tons, is on the point of sailing from Deptford, for the new colony of Georgia, with 35 families, consisting of Carpenters, Bricklayers, Farmers, Etc. who take all proper Instruments. The men were learning Military Discipline of the Guards, as must all that go thither, and to carry Musquets, Bayonets, and Swords, to defend the Colony in case of an Attack from the Indians. She has on board 10 Tun of Alderman Parson's best Beer, and will take in at the Maderas 5 Tun of Wine, for the service of the Colony. James Oglethorpe Esq., one of the Trustees, goes with them to see them settled.'

The colony was soon established and James Oglethorpe was re-

Westbrook, Godalming, the country seat of James Oglethorpe, founder of the State of Georgia in 1732.

sponsible for the laying out of its capital, Savannah. The Indians he befriended and the real threat to the new colony came from the Spanish in Florida to the south. However, his qualities as a soldier were seen to full effect and Georgia was successfully defended.

In 1734 Oglethorpe returned to England and brought with him ten Indians of the Yamacraw tribe, including their chief, Tomochichi. The appearance of the Indians caused quite a stir and people came from many miles around to see them at The White Hart in Godalming's High Street. Unfortunately, this was the time of one of the great smallpox epidemics in the town and when one of the Indians caught the dread disease and died, the others isolated themselves in Oglethorpe's house.

In October 1735, Oglethorpe sailed again for his colony, taking with him the Wesley brothers, John and Charles. Further war with Spain threatened the future of Georgia but a campaign against larger forces pushed back the enemy and ensured the safety of his infant colony. Much of the cost of the war had been met from Oglethorpe's own funds but the Treasury refused to reimburse all of the expenditure, with the result that he had to mortgage Westbrook to stave off bankruptcy.

In February 1743 Oglethorpe was promoted to the rank of brigadier-general and later in the same year he returned to England, leaving the colony which he had so successfully founded for ever. He had intended to come to England to raise more troops to defend Georgia, but the Jacobite Rising of 1745 intervened to upset his plans and he and his soldiers were diverted to join the Duke of Cumberland, whose forces were harassing the retreating Jacobites. Oglethorpe and the Duke were totally incompatible characters and such was the Duke's dislike for his fellow soldier, born, no doubt, from jealousy of the other's obviously superior talent, that he lodged a charge of misconduct. An apocryphal story, which was current at the time, claimed that Oglethorpe had been caught on the eve of Culloden in possession of 'treasonable correspondence' and had fled to Westbrook. There he proceeded to fortify his house with a crenellated wall guarded by small forts. One of these forts survives to this day on the hillside above Westbrook, but it was almost certainly built by Oglethorpe's sister, Anne, a known Jacobite sympathiser, at a time when he was still in Georgia.

Although acquitted at the court-martial, Oglethorpe's soldiering days were at an end. He had already solved his financial problems by marriage to an heiress and he now actively resumed his role as MP for Haslemere. He became a friend of Dr Johnson and Boswell and lived out the remainder of his life uneventfully until he died in 1785.

The first house at Claremont, near Esher, was built by Sir John Vanbrugh, the famous architect and playwright, for his own use. Whilst somewhat smaller than the famous Blenheim Palace and Castle Howard, which he also designed, it was still an imposing crenellated mansion with seven acres of gardens enclosed by a substantial brick wall. Vanbrugh called it his 'very small box' but chose the site because he found it 'singularly romantick'. In 1714 he sold the house to Thomas Pelham, who later became the Duke of Newcastle and was Prime Minister under both George II and George III. Vanbrugh now altered the façade of the house for its new owner and added two large wings. It was here in his fine mansion that Newcastle entertained the royal family, politicians like Sir Robert Walpole and, it is said, the exile Voltaire.

Claremont, built for Lord Clive of India by 'Capability' Brown in the late 1760s. It replaced an earlier house designed by Sir John Vanbrugh.

The arrival of Queen Victoria and Prince Albert at Claremont. The dog in the foreground is almost certainly the Queen's favourite greyhound, Eos.

The gardens at Claremont were originally geometrically formal, with straight rows of trees and a round pond. Newcastle considerably extended the grounds and had an amphitheatre, particularly for cock-fighting, built to the north-west of the pond with a magnificent belvedere on a hillock to the west of the house. The latter still survives. Newcastle then turned to the increasingly fashionable William Kent, the pioneer of naturalistic landscape gardening, who redesigned much of the garden. He turned the formal pond into a lake with an island, upon which he built a domed pavilion. At one end of the lake he created a naturalistic grotto decorated with stalactites and crystals.

When the Duke of Newcastle died in 1768, Claremont was sold to Lord Clive, who had returned from India in 1766, having successfully fought a series of military campaigns which had added the great subcontinent to the growing British Empire. Clive soon sent for Lancelot 'Capability' Brown, Kent's former pupil, and commissioned him to demolish Vanbrugh's house and build another on adjacent higher ground. With the help of his partner, Henry Holland, and also a youthful John Soane, later Sir John, the museum founder, Capability Brown built a magnificent mansion with commanding views over the neighbouring countryside. He also remodelled the grounds, but retained some of Kent's features, such as the lake and its island temple. In total,

The Duchess of Albany with two of her grandchildren – she was the wife of Queen Victoria's youngest son, Leopold, and lived for many years at Claremont.

the work at Claremont is estimated to have cost Lord Clive £100,000. But he had little opportunity to savour it.

During the rebuilding of Claremont, Clive's life became increasingly troubled by accusations and rumour. He was said to have gained his riches in India by accepting bribes, but he rebutted his accusers by claiming that much of his wealth had come from gifts honestly received. In addition to these problems, Clive's health was also failing fast and for much of the time he was in constant pain, relieved only by increasing amounts of opium. In 1774, shunned and vilified by those who had once feted him as a hero, he took his own life at his house in London.

On 2nd May 1816 Princess Charlotte, daughter of the Prince Regent, later George IV, married Prince Leopold of Saxe-Coburg. The following month a bill was passed by Parliament for the purchase of Claremont as a gift from the nation to the young couple. Thus, for a brief period, Claremont became the focus of the country's attention following Wellington's glorious final victory over Napoleon at Waterloo. Charlotte was a well-educated, popular young woman, fond of music and poetry, whose own adaptation of a poem by Thompson says much for the image of Surrey current at the time:

> 'To Claremont's terraced heights and Esher's groves,
> Where in the sweetest solitude embraced
> By the soft winding of the silent Mole,
> From courts and cities Charlotte finds repose
> Enchanting vale! beyond whate'er the Muse
> Has of Acjaia or Hespera sung:
> O, vale of bliss! O, softly swelling hills,
> On which the power of cultivation lies,
> And joys to see the wonder of his toil.'

Charlotte's birthday on 11th February 1817 was a day of much rejoicing locally. Esher was decorated with flags and bunting and parties were the order of the day. In celebration, the royal couple gave £100 to improve the lot of the local poor and an illuminated Claremont shone like a beacon over the surrounding countryside.

There were many famous visitors to the house during Charlotte and Leopold's ownership, including the Duke of Wellington, Grand Duke Nicholas of Russia, later Tsar Nicholas, and the Duke and Duchess of Orleans, who were living in exile at Twickenham at the time. Just over 30 years later the Duke was to return to Claremont, as the deposed King Louis Philippe, where he lived out his second exile in England and died in 1850. Charlotte and Leopold lived quietly away from the machinations of the royal court. Leopold's great friend, Dr Stockmar, wrote that 'in this house reign harmony, peace and love – in short everthing that can promote domestic happiness.' It was not to last – on 17th November 1817, Charlotte died at Claremont, having given birth to a stillborn son. The nation was devastated and Leopold heartbroken. He continued to live at Claremont, leaving everything as it had been in Charlotte's time, until he was elected King of the Belgians in 1831.

Leopold was the uncle of Princess Victoria, daughter of the Duke of Kent, who spent much of her childhood at Claremont. Many years later, Queen Victoria was to remember her days there with fond affection. 'Claremont remains as the brightest epoch of my otherwise melancholy childhood', she wrote in 1872. During the early days of her reign, Victoria and Prince Albert often came from Windsor to stay at Claremont. In January 1843 she wrote to Leopold, 'I am happy to write to you again from this very dear and comfortable place [which] has a peculiar charm for us both, and to me it brings back recollections of the happiest days of my otherwise dull childhood – where I experienced such kindness from you, dearest Uncle, which has ever since continued.'

Claremont later became the home of Victoria's youngest son, the Duke of Albany, named Leopold after his more famous uncle. The Duke died in 1884 but his wife remained at Claremont for many years. She was a popular figure in Surrey, always ready to drive out to the four corners of the county to open a new school or institution. Part of the gardens of Claremont were restored a few years ago and are open to the public. Clive's house became a school in 1931, a role which has so far ensured the survival of this fine 18th century mansion.

It was inevitable that those who could not afford the luxury of a country seat like Claremont would aspire to achieve the next best thing. This is reflected in the surviving smaller houses of the period, especially in the towns. The best examples are to be found among the many Georgian town houses in Farnham. The town grew rich on the profits of its extensive corn market and was also surrounded by fields of some of the best hops to be grown anywhere in England. The finest of its houses are in West Street, particularly Wilmer House, built in 1718 and now the town museum, and the adjacent Sandford House of 1757.

When an owner could not afford to rebuild his property in the latest Georgian style, he might resort to the trick of refronting his existing house in brick. Therefore, many a 'Georgian' house in towns such as Godalming, Guildford and Reigate, in fact, hides timber-framing of a much earlier period. Meanwhile, the more humble of the people lived on in those small cottages of timber, wattle and daub, now so beloved by the 20th century commuter.

13

CHANGE IN THE COUNTRYSIDE

As the influence of London spread further out into Surrey there was one problem which hampered the growth of prosperity in the towns and villages – the poor condition of the roads, especially across those areas of clay both to the north and south of the Downs. In winter these unsurfaced tracks were reduced to a quagmire unless set hard by a sharp frost. When the Duke of Richmond travelled through Surrey to his country seat at Goodwood he needed eight horses to pull his coach, in order to be certain of getting through. For the Duke of Somerset the average speed of the trip to his seat at Petworth was less than two miles an hour. Little surprise, therefore, that in each town and village along these routes there developed a plethora of stopping places in the form of inns and taverns. The Duke of Somerset would break his journey with a stopover at his own town house in Guildford. The Duke of Richmond often did the same at Godalming.

The improvement of the road system throughout the county was an important feature of the second half of the 18th century and the early part of the following century. It was achieved by the establishment of turnpike trusts responsible for the upkeep of the roads in return for the payment of tolls by those using them. Tollgates, with their cottages for the collector, soon became a feature of these turnpike roads.

There were several important main routes which traversed the county. They included the road from London to Portsmouth by way of Kingston, Esher, Cobham, Ripley, Guildford and Godalming and out over the heights of Hindhead and into Hampshire. At Cobham there was a mile stretch of road running straight and true across a well drained gravel plateau. Here the coaches got up a good speed, perhaps 20 miles an hour, and for this reason the stretch became known as the Fairmile, a name which has survived to this day. The route from Kingston to Sheet, near Petersfield was turnpiked in 1758 and further improved in 1826. Turnpike improvements such as these often left sections of the old road abandoned, which can still be traced where the former route

The Tadworth tollgate on the turnpike to Reigate.

has survived as a bridleway or track. Thus, at Hindhead, the old route went right over Hind Common on the very lip of the Devil's Punchbowl. To remove the steep climb which considerably slowed down the coaches, a new road was constructed in 1826 some way down the slope. It is this route which the A3 follows at the time of writing. However, the ultimate in road improvements is soon scheduled for this area, where it is planned to put the road through a tunnel dug under the hill. The original road traversed by the likes of Samuel Pepys is now nothing more than a rough track between the gorse and bracken.

In East Surrey the most important route ran through Croydon and then up the Caterham Valley and over the Downs to Godstone. The road then went straight over Tilburstow Hill and down into Sussex, where it gave access to the ancient ports of Lewes and Shoreham. Later, when sea bathing became popular, the route was improved to provide a good road to Brighton, by the removal of difficult sections such as the steep climb over Tilburstow Hill. Another route to Brighton came over the Downs at Tadworth to Reigate. Most of this route was turnpiked for carriages in 1755 and further improved in 1820 – improvements which considerably eased the gradient of Reigate Hill and also gave travellers coming from London that abrupt entry into the town of Reigate via a tunnel, an excitement lost to the car driver only in recent years.

The great coaching days were ended by the railways but up to the First World War there was an enthusiasts' revival. This is the American Alfred Vanderbilt's coach in Reigate about 1910. Vanderbilt was drowned when the *Lusitania* was torpedoed in 1915.

In the mid-1750s a new turnpike road was built connecting Epsom with Guildford, which for much of its route ran along the edge of the Downs on well drained land. For some time it was a more popular road for travellers from Kingston to Guildford via Leatherhead than the more direct but poorer road via Esher and Ripley.

These improvements to the roads were potentially a great boost to the prosperity of Surrey's farmers, for the rapidly expanding markets of London were now much more readily accessible. The 18th century saw many improvements in the county's agriculture. Market gardens were established in the northern parts of the county to supply fresh vegetables to the capital. In the Woking and Chertsey areas the soil proved highly suitable for the cultivation of root crops such as parsnips and carrots. Potatoes also became a popular crop, which found a ready market in London. New studies of farming methods led to the introduction in many parts of Surrey of a better system of crop rotation. In medieval times perhaps one third of the land would be lying fallow, but the planting of new varieties of grass and root crops such as turnips removed the necessity of this wastage. These crops also provided better fodder for cattle and sheep, especially through the winter, enabling farmers to keep more animals into the following year, thus expanding the size of their herds and flocks. Some areas on the North Downs, particularly Banstead, were famous for the quality of the mutton from the local sheep. However, over the greater part of the county, arable predominated over pasture and the growing of wheat, barley and oats was the main farming activity.

The population of England is estimated to have been about six million in 1760 but by 1831 it had more than doubled. With such a rapidly expanding market for their produce the landowners and farmers of Surrey were under pressure to improve their methods to increase production. However, there were still factors which considerably hindered the improvement of the county's agricultural output. In many parts of Surrey the inefficient medieval system of strip cultivation in common fields survived into the 19th century. For example, there were 300 acres of such fields in Egham parish, 250 acres in adjacent Hythe, 2,000 in Sutton and Cheam and the same number in Leatherhead. Enclosure was seen by many as the panacea.

Those intent on improvement also looked avariciously upon the county's 17,500 acres of commons, where farmers and villagers exercised their ancient commoners' rights to graze their animals, dig peat and turf for fuel and cut wood. William Stevenson in his 1809 report on the state of the county's agriculture wrote of 'the situation and extent of wastes, commons and common fields in Surrey, the nature of the soil of each, the loss and disgrace attending their present state, and the advantage that would result to the landed proprietors, the farmers, and the country at large, if they were brought into proper cultivation.' It was often the nature of the soil that limited agricultural development, but even the county's 48,000 acres of acid heathlands came under Stevenson's scrutiny and were deemed suitable for the growing of fir trees. So gradually, the remaining common fields were enclosed and the more fertile commons fenced off, leaving those of limited income and resources bereft of rights which had once kept them just above the poverty line. For many people, as these oft quoted lines from *The Tickler Magazine* of February 1802 made clear, enclosure was nothing short of legalised robbery:

> 'The fault is great in man or woman
> Who steals a goose from off the common,
> But what can plead THAT man
> Who steals a common off a goose?'

A champion of the dispossessed farmer was William Cobbett, who was born in 1763 at Farnham and died at Normandy, near Ash, in 1835. Cobbett was a prolific writer and political commentator who spent a number of years in America. When he returned to England he was appalled to find the dramatic changes which were taking place in the countryside he loved. He particularly hated to see the growth of London, the 'great wen', as he called the capital, and he spent much of the latter part of his life in outspoken criticism of those who saw the countryside only as a source of profit.

Cobbett is best remembered for his book *Rural Rides*, which resulted from a tour he made on horseback through substantial areas of England, mainly in the 1820s. Cobbett wanted to see for himself how the people of the countryside were faring, to use his travels as a vehicle for his political views and often to comment on the farms and crops which he passed by on his route.

In September 1826 Cobbett was at Worcester, where the hop harvest had recently been completed. There he met a man who claimed that he would never use Farnham hops in brewing, even if they were a gift. Cobbett, uncharacteristically not wishing to get into an argument on this score, simply noted that 'Farnham hops always sold at about double the price of the Worcester; but if he had said the same thing to any other Farnham man that I ever saw, I should have preferred being absent from the spot: the hops are bitter, but nothing is their bitterness compared to the language that my townsman would have put forth.'

Cobbett did not exaggerate the comparison between the Farnham and Worcester hops, for those grown on the sheltered hillsides around his home town were considered by brewers to be amongst the very best. Hop growing was well established around Farnham by the beginning of the 18th century, when there were an estimated 300 acres of gardens. Towards the end of the century, paler, bitter beers began to become fashionable and the lighter coloured Farnham hop became particularly favoured. This popularity was reflected in a rapid increase in the extent of the gardens, which had reached nearly 1,000 acres by 1841. From 1774 all hops were required by law to be packed in special bags or 'pockets' marked with the year of growth, the place and name of the grower. In Farnham the pockets were stamped with a great variety of insignia identifying individual growers. The hops were sold each October at the great hop fair at Weyhill in Hampshire, where the Farnham sellers had their own stand and where, as Cobbett noted, their hops invariably obtained the best prices. One place in Surrey which Cobbett does not seem to have visited, perhaps because it was too close to his hated 'great wen', was the 'physic' gardens of Mitcham. Which is a pity,

Cutting lavender in the fields near Wallington in about 1905.

because they were once a particularly fascinating part of the county's agricultural scene.

The soil of the area around Mitcham was described as a 'rich black mould' and was particularly favourable for the cultivation of a variety of important herbs, of which lavender and peppermint were the most important. 'Mitcham mints' have remained popular well into the 20th century, but the plant was also used in the manufacture of peppermint water or cordial. Lavender growing at Mitcham possibly dates from medieval years and was well established by Cobbett's time. Rapid expansion took place in the early 19th century and, by the 1850s, there were over 800 acres of 'physic' gardens in the area. Here many other plants with a variety of uses, especially in medicines, were also grown. These included camomile, poppy, liquorice, rhubarb, mint, aniseed and wormwood. Such was the demand during Victorian times that the gardens, especially for lavender, soon spread out from Mitcham to take in many acres of fields around Carshalton, Beddington, Wallington and Sutton.

The harvesting of the various herbs required a great deal of extra labour. Often the children were kept home from school, according to the season, to help in the gathering of the camomile, peppermint or lavender. As a result, absenteeism was a serious problem in many Mitcham schools and prizes were offered for record attendance as an encouragement to put school first. Many Irish families would come to help when the lavender and peppermint was harvested, afterwards travelling on to Kent for the hop-picking. Lavender oil was extracted in distilleries and these usually two-storey wooden buildings were once a common sight around Mitcham. The stills themselves were huge copper vessels. Schoolboys were often employed to tread down the flowers in them and sometimes paid danger money in a good season for bees! Apparently, after a few days of treading, the boys became oblivious to the pain.

The decline of this remarkable industry around Mitcham belongs to a later phase of Surrey's history, when the flower-covered fields were smothered by suburban housing and the once perfumed air replaced by the smoke of a mass of domestic chimneys.

By the 1850s, when the physic gardens of Mitcham were in their prime, the lot of those who toiled in the fields of Surrey was still one of hard labour and an uncertain future. Matters had improved a little from the bad times of the Napoleonic Wars and their aftermath. In those days the poverty of the farm labourer and his family had been inextricably linked to the quality of each corn harvest and the resultant price of bread, their staple food. When the harvest was poor, the labourer found his wages cut or he was laid off without any pay at all. At the same time, food shortages, against a background of rapidly rising population, pushed up demand, causing higher prices. Therefore, the gap between what the labourer had to spend and the price of the food he needed to buy, to avoid starvation, widened dramatically. Even men in full employment often failed to earn sufficient to feed their growing families.

The Poor Laws instituted towards the end of the reign of Elizabeth I had worked reasonably well whilst the population remained relatively stable. There had been changes over the years – in 1723 parish officers were empowered to set up workhouses in which to lodge the poor and set them to useful employment. Many Surrey parishes established workhouses as a result and in 1782 parishes were allowed to operate joint workhouses. However, by the end of the Napoleonic Wars in 1815, the demands of the poor rate, levied on the owners of property and land for the upkeep of the parish poor, began to place a heavy burden upon the more well-off parishioners. This is well illustrated in Shere, which in the late Georgian period was still a fairly isolated rural community. In 1780 only 88 out of a total of about 820 inhabitants of the parish were receiving poor relief. By 1818/1819 the population had risen by a little over 200, yet 554 were being supported from the poor rate. However, the Shere overseers did not shirk their responsibilities in looking after the health and welfare of their less fortunate parishioners – as this entry in their accounts dated 14th October 1821 proves:

'James Tickner, for sea bathing at Margate, £5'

Sea bathing was at the time, of course, considered highly beneficial for the cure of a great variety of ailments. In James Tickner's case it seems to have worked, although there is no record of what he was actually suffering from. Such care cost money, which in 1780 in Shere had amounted to £155 but this had risen to £1,138 by 1818/1819.

Clearly economies of scale were what was called for. The result was the Poor Law Amendment Act of 1834, which grouped large numbers of parishes together in 'unions' with a single workhouse. The affairs of the poor were now to be looked after by a 'board of guardians' and efficiency and a reduction in the poor rate was the main objective, not an improvement in the lot of the poor. Shere found itself in the Guildford Union, whose workhouse in Warren Road, Guildford, was opened in 1838. For the poor of the village, especially those suffering the infirmity of old age, it was a long way from home.

14

THE INDUSTRIES OF SURREY

The improvement in communications in Surrey during the reign of George III was not confined to the turnpiking of the county's roads. Several canals were also constructed, which gave producers of a variety of bulk goods and foodstuffs access to greatly expanded markets. Guildford and those places along the lower reaches of the river Wey had experienced the advantages of water transport since 1653, when the Wey Navigation was opened. This linked the county town with the Thames, giving access not only to London but also upstream as far as Oxford. The driving force behind this pioneering waterway was Sir Richard Weston of Sutton Place. He had witnessed the operation of pound locks and sluices in the Netherlands and is credited with introducing the system to England. As a result of this remarkable feat of engineering, Guildford developed into an important centre for the supply of corn and timber, mainly oak from the Wealden woodlands, to London. Guildford beer was also much in demand in the capital and barges laden with barrels were a frequent sight upon the river.

In the spring of 1764 this waterway was extended to Godalming, with the opening of the Godalming Navigation. The Wey Navigation had brought barges only as far as the downstream side of Guildford's Town Bridge. The central arch of the medieval bridge was now enlarged and a further series of locks constructed, to enable barges to proceed to a wharf at Godalming. Here a busy centre for the bulk shipment of corn, timber, iron and stone was quickly developed.

In 1794 the Basingstoke Canal was opened, which, leaving the Wey a short distance downstream from Byfleet, ran north of the old settlement of Woking and Pirbright to Frimley and Ash. Its course then went out of the county into Hampshire, south of the small village of Aldershot and thence to Basingstoke. The Surrey section of the canal required 28 locks and a cutting through Frimley Hill 1,000 yards long and up to 70 ft deep. The cutting gave the name of Deepcut to the adjacent area. It was intended that the canal should then link up with the Itchen, giving

Ash Vale Boathouse on the Basingstoke Canal in about 1910.

an inland waterway to Southampton, but this extension was never built. Thus, traffic on the canal was limited and it never made a profit, despite receiving a boost when Aldershot was developed as a military base in the late 1850s. A small amount of commercial traffic continued on the Surrey section of the Basingstoke Canal until 1949, when a last load of timber was carried to Woking. The canal was then left to decay until 1966 when a group of enthusiasts formed the Surrey and Hampshire Canal Society to press for restoration. Surrey and Hampshire County Councils purchased the canal during the 1970s. Since then, a workforce consisting mainly of volunteers has restored the canal through much of its length, aided by money from the councils, local companies and private donations.

The Wey and Arun Junction Canal was opened in 1816 to provide a link between the Godalming Navigation near Shalford and the Arun Canal at Newbridge, near Wisborough Green in Sussex. It thus completed the inland waterway linking London with the English Channel and ran via Bramley to Alfold, then into Sussex at Loxwood. The Surrey section required 15 locks and a small aqueduct at Bramley. Barges on the canal carried a great variety of goods – seaweed, for use as fertilizer, coal, groceries and provisions were brought from Littlehampton, whilst timber, flour, bark and farm produce were carried away. Very occasionally, barges passed through under heavy guard,

118

carrying bullion to the Bank of England. Like so many canals throughout Britain, it was the coming of the railways which killed off this waterway and in 1871 it closed. Since 1970 there have been valiant efforts to restore it and some sections have been reclaimed but, as parts of the canal bed are now built over, it seems unlikely that it can ever be returned to its former glory.

It would be easy to believe that, apart from these interesting canals, the county of Surrey has little to contribute to the industrial heritage of Britain. Nothing could be further from the truth. The industries of the county are worthy of a substantial history of their own, but here there is space for only a brief résumé, with examples, to give a hint of a complex and varied past.

During the medieval period, the south-west of the county developed into a centre for the production of woollen cloth. It is said that the monks of Waverley Abbey, founded in 1128, were responsible for the beginnings of the industry, which was centred on the three main settlements of Farnham, Guildford and Godalming. The hills around the area, with their mainly light soils, were ideal for the folding of sheep, and the chalk downs in particular offered good grass upon which the animals thrived. The river and streams provided a steady head of water to drive the fulling mills, fulling being an important process in the manufacture of the cloth, when the raw woven material was cleansed and thickened in a mixture of water and fuller's earth. Fuller's earth occurs as a natural substance in geological deposits of the Cretaceous age, especially at Nutfield near Reigate. In modern times the earth has been dug for a great variety of other uses, with 40% of it being used as cat litter. The deposits have now been worked out and the last pit closed only recently.

Originally, fulling was done by men treading or walking the cloth in wooden tubs filled with the fuller's earth and water. It is from this occupation that the common surname of 'Walker' is derived. Sometime in the first half of the 13th century the power of the waterwheel was harnessed to drive large wooden mallets which pummelled the cloth, thus making Mr Walker redundant. Many watermills in Surrey were used for fulling at some point in their history – one of the earliest in England was built at Guildford in 1251. During the 14th century there was a fulling mill at Catteshall, near Godalming, and Rake Mill at Milford was recorded as one in 1577.

Cloth manufacture in south-west Surrey was well established by 1252. In that year it was recorded that 'Chalons of Guildford', a type of cloth named after Chalon-sur-Marne in France, was bought for Henry III at Winchester Fair. By the reign of Elizabeth I production was concentrated

Sheep shearing at Leigh in 1908. At the height of the prosperity of the Surrey woollen industry in the 16th century this would have been a common sight in the Surrey countryside.

on a type of course cloth called 'Kersey' from the town of that name in Suffolk, where it originated. The cloth was commonly dyed blue with woad, and became known generically as 'Guildford Blue', although much of it was made in adjacent places, particularly Godalming, Wonersh and outlying villages such as Horsley.

After the fulling process was completed, the lengths of cloth were stretched and dried on racks or tenter-frames, being fixed to the device by tenterhooks. This process has left its legacy in the English language with the phrase 'to be on tenterhooks'. Racks were to be found in various places in Godalming, whilst in Guildford the industry is still recalled by the name of Racks Close, near the Castle. The process gave the unscrupulous clothier the opportunity to make larger profits by over stretching the cloth during drying, thereby producing greater lengths for the same original amount of material. The buyer would not, of course, be aware of the trick until the cloth next got wet! In 1391 Parliament passed a statute in an attempt to combat the abuse, but the problem continued to regularly occur. In 1565 twelve Godalming clothiers were accused of using various instruments to strain and stretch their cloth.

It was this dishonesty which many saw as the main cause of the rapid decline of the industry during the reign of James I. Although it was, perhaps, partly to blame, the real reason was that this rather coarse cloth had simply become unfashionable in the face of competition from finer weaves. By the end of the 17th century the cloth industry had died out completely in Farnham, Guildford and Wonersh, but John Aubrey, writing in the late 1670s, was able to say of Godalming, 'This town is eminent for Clothing, the most of any Place in this County: Here they maked mix'd Kersies, and blue Kersies for the Canaries, which for their Colour are not equall'd by any in England.' The curious destination of the cloth is probably explained by the fact that the Canary Islands acted as a staging post for distribution throughout the Spanish Empire in the New World. Clothmaking survived on a much reduced scale in the town until well into the Victorian period.

In Godalming, as the cloth industry fell from importance it was replaced by the framework knitting of hosiery. The town become a major centre for the production of stockings and other knitted items in wool, silk and cotton. A major development occurred in 1788, when George Holland was granted a patent for the manufacture, from specially prepared wool, of 'Fleecy and Segovia Hosiery'. Godalming was quickly established as the centre of production for Holland's hosiery, which was described in the patent as a 'new invented method of making stockings, gloves, mitts, socks, caps, coats, waistcoats, breeches, cloaks, and other clothing, and linings for the same, for persons afflicted with gout, rheumatism, and other complaints requiring warmth, and of common use in cold climates, and of making false or downy calves in stockings, a thing never before put in practise.' Production of George Holland's invention continued in Godalming until about 1890, but other branches of the knitting industry continued to operate in the town until very recently. Two Victorian hosiery factory buildings survive today, as does does a fine

A knitting frame. A similar frame can be seen in Godalming Museum.

A papermill at Chilworth in about 1850, with St Martha's church prominent in the background. (Surrey Archaeological Society)

example of a frameshop in Mint Street – reminders of a once important Surrey industry.

There were many other industries in Surrey which, like clothmaking, had need of a good water supply and power from the waterwheel. These included, for example, papermaking and tanning. There were papermills on several of the county's rivers including the river Wey and the Tillingbourne, where high quality paper for banknotes was manufactured. Tanneries were also to be found in a number of places along these rivers. Calico bleaching and snuff manufacture were amongst many industries active on the river Wandle, but perhaps the most fascinating industry of all was the manufacture of gunpowder, especially on the river Tillingbourne.

William Cobbett, referring to one of his numerous rides along the Tillingbourne valley wrote, 'I came over the high hill on the south of Guildford, and came down to Chilworth, and up the valley to Albury. I noticed, in my first Rural Ride, this beautiful valley, its hangers, its meadows, its hop-gardens, and its ponds . . . This pretty valley of Chilworth has a run of water which comes out of the high hills, and which, occasionally, spreads into a pond . . . This valley, which seems to have been created by bountiful providence, as one of the choicest retreats of man; which seems formed for a scene of innocence and happiness, has been, by ungrateful man, so perverted as to make it instrumental in effecting two of the most damnable of purposes; in carrying into execution two of the damnable inventions that ever sprang from the minds of man under the influence of the devil! namely, the making of *gunpowder* and of *banknotes!*'

In Surrey the story of the first of these 'damnable inventions' begins well before Cobbett's time. In 1589 the Evelyn family of Wotton were granted patents by Elizabeth I for the manufacture of gunpowder. It is thought that their original powdermill was at Long Ditton and later at Godstone, whilst at Abinger a mill was operated by one of the Evelyns' partners, Richard Hill. In 1625 the first powdermill at Chilworth was established by the East India Company. The Company had the advantage of a supply of natural saltpetre, that essential ingredient of gunpowder, which they imported from the sub-continent in large quantities. Here, beside the rippling, clear waters of Surrey's most picturesque stream, there developed one of the nation's most important centres of gunpowder manufacture.

Martin Tupper, the Victorian poet and author who lived nearby at Albury, described the Chilworth powdermills and their visual effect upon the countryside in a poem written in the 1840s:

'Mammon, from those long white mills
With foggy steam the prospect fills;
Chimneys red with sulph'rous smoke
Blight those hanging groves of oak.'

Down in the 'long white mills' precautions were stringent and workers wore special clothing and shoes without metal studs – and with good cause, for the slightest spark could blow everything to kingdom come. And at Chilworth, with ominous regularity, it did. There were fatal explosions at the works in 1864, 1874, 1879 and 1883, but the worst tragedy was the loss of six men in the 'Great Explosion' in 1901.

At twenty minutes to nine on that frosty morning in February, the chill air above the village of Chilworth was rent by two tremendous explosions. Smoke shot high into the sky and bricks, sheets of corrugated iron, baulks of timber, machinery and the remains of the unfortunate workers were tossed in all directions. Three men had been loading a tramway trolley outside a building known as the black corning house, where gunpowder in cake form was crushed and granulated into powder. Three more men were working inside the house. It is thought that a spark ignited the powder on the trolley, which exploded and set off a further blast that demolished the adjacent building. The recovery of the bodies was a grisly affair, for they had been scattered over an area up to 150 yards away from where the men had been working.

The memory of this tragedy lingered long after the closure of the powdermills in 1922. Some ruins remain of this hellish place, now tranquil and green, and in the village itself there still survive some workmen's cottages, their front doors opening straight out onto the pavement, reminiscent of industrial towns of northern England.

Surrey has a varied geology and, as a result, a long history of quarrying and mining for stone, clay and gravel. In addition, the county has a tradition of iron working, which possibly goes back more than 2,000 years, but reached its zenith during the reign of James I. The Wealden iron industry existed along much of the southern border of the county by medieval times and extended well into Sussex, where it was much more extensive. The iron ore came from small opencast pits dug into beds of the Lower Cretaceous age and was mainly in the form of a clay ironstone. At some places in the county the ground is still pockmarked with the collapsed remains of these 'bell' pits. Other low grade ores were also sometimes used, such as an ironstone known locally as 'carstone', which occurs in the 'Folkstone Beds' of the Lower Greensand.

The iron was smelted using charcoal produced in the Wealden woods. Charcoal was known as coal in those days and those who produced it were colliers, which introduced another fairly common English surname. The name was later transferred to those who mined 'sea coal', as mineral coal was then called. The demand for charcoal was so great during the 16th century that the woodlands were seriously threatened. It is safe to say that today there are more trees in the Surrey countryside than there were in 1600.

Until about 1500 the iron was smelted using small furnaces or 'bloomeries' which produced irregular masses of iron bloom, which were then beaten with hammers. Originally, the hammering was done manually, but during the 15th century the power of the waterwheel was first used to drive mechanical hammers, which pounded the iron into solid bars. Bloomery sites have been discovered at Lingfield, Godstone, Leigh and Thursley. There is documentary evidence for other sites at Charlwood, Newdigate and near Horley. The name 'Abinger Hammer' is a reminder that the industry once existed there. Numerous attractive ponds in other southern parts of the county are thought to have originated as hammer ponds. Here the water was penned up to provide the fall to drive the waterwheel, which powered the hammers.

About 1600, the blast furnace was introduced from the Continent and the waterwheel was additionally used to drive mechanical bellows, which replaced the inefficient foot bellows of the bloomeries. Ironworks were established at many places, like Imbhams, near Haslemere, where guns

An earthenware shop at Farnham, sketched by Thomas Rowlandson in 1782. Undoubtedly the products sold here would have been of local manufacture.

and shot were being cast at the start of the Civil War. Throughout south Surrey the woodlands were being rapidly consumed by the insatiable demand of the furnaces and pressure was increasing to prevent further growth of the industry. Several statutes were passed by Parliament in an attempt to control the felling of woodland, which the government saw as an important source of timber for ship building. These pressures, coupled with the fact that the best ironstone deposits were becoming worked out, brought the heyday of Surrey's iron industry to an end. In addition, better grades of ore had been found in the Midlands, near to good supplies of coal, which had first been used in smelting in 1620.

Another important Surrey industry, which also consumed large quantities of timber, was glassmaking. Glassmakers were working in the woods of south-west Surrey soon after 1300, and possibly even earlier. Some of the makers were local people, but there were also foreigners who, certainly from the mid-16th century, introduced improved methods of manufacture. These glassworks produced domestic vessels, phials, apothecaries' wares and window glass. In 1352 John de Alemaygne of Chiddingfold supplied large quantities of glass for St Stephen's Chapel at Westminster. In 1356 the same maker also supplied glass for the windows of St George's Chapel at Windsor. These glassmakers made use of local materials – sand, potash produced from coppice-wood and bracken, and oak to fire the furnace. Local malmstone, also known as

125

The entrance to a hearthstone mine near Marden Park, Godstone, photographed on 16th June 1900. The well-dressed lady is not a mineworker but a member of a party from the Geologists' Association!

firestone, was used for the furnace floor because of its heat resistant properties. The clay for the all important crucible was probably brought in from elsewhere.

A glasshouse site near Hambledon has been excavated by archaeologists and dated to about 1330. The remains of two crude furnaces were uncovered – the larger was interpreted as a melting furnace, whilst the smaller one was probably used for other processes such as annealing. Both furnaces had been housed in a wooden building roofed with tiles, of which only a few postholes and broken tiles remained.

In the mid-16th century glass production was greatly expanded and, whilst it continued in Surrey, the main centre seems to have shifted slightly south to Wisborough Green, across the border in Sussex. Several glassmakers from France came to work in the area, including John Carré from Arras and Isaac Bougard, or Bungar. The remains of a glasshouse of this period were discovered in Sidney Wood near Alfold in the mid-1960s. Here archaeologists led by Eric Wood excavated a series of rectangular furnaces, including a sophisticated double chambered annealing furnace, so far unique in Britain. The products made here included window glass, drinking glasses, bottles, distilling apparatus, domestic ware such as bowls, plates and hour-glasses, and medical ware including urinals (so called because physicians of the time determined the state of health of their patients by studying the colour of their urine in these bottles). The high cost of fuel in Surrey, mainly due to the competition for the limited supply from ironmakers, brought about a rapid decline in the Surrey glass industry during the reign of James I. The last glassmaker in the area was Isaac Bungar, who finally gave up the struggle in 1618. Sir Robert Mansell had obtained the monopoly for a coal-fired glassmaking process and it was this which finally drove poor Isaac out of business.

The best outcrops for firestone are in East Surrey, where there exist in many places labyrinths of underground tunnels and caverns excavated over several centuries for the stone. Although much used where a heat resistant stone was required, such as in furnaces and fireplaces, it was also extensively employed as building stone. Known also as Reigate Stone, there is evidence for its use in Saxon churches. Later, in 1259, stone from Merstham and Reigate was supplied in large quantities for the building of the Royal Palace at Westminster. It was used in the 14th century at Windsor Castle and also at Hampton Court and Oatlands Palace two centuries later. The stone could be intricately carved and was much used inside buildings and for window tracery. It was not so successful for external work, being prone to frost scaling, as can be clearly seen on the outside walls of Reigate parish church. Another product of the mines was a soft friable sandstone called hearthstone, which was used to whiten hearths, doorsteps and stone floors. The latter was the sole output of the three mines still working in 1931, but the last mine closed in 1961, thus ending over 1,000 years of mining history.

A large number of other mineral resources have been extracted from beneath the soil of Surrey over the centuries. In the Godalming area there are Lower Greensand deposits of Bargate Stone, which were once extensively quarried. This stone was used during the Iron Age, the Roman period and in a large variety of buildings from the medieval period onwards. It occurs as large masses, called by the quarrymen 'doggers', in an otherwise soft sand, and was extracted from the quarry face using a unique method known as 'jumping a stone'. An iron block was used as a pivot for a long crowbar, which was placed under one end of the stone to be dug out. A plank was then placed at right angles on the opposite end of the crowbar. Several men, using long poles to balance themselves, then jumped up and down on the plank in unison. This process gradually loosened the 'dogger' from the quarry face. Like the firestone mines, all the Bargate Stone quarries have now closed. In later years the stone was crushed for use as road metalling, but proved too soft for the wear and tear of modern traffic.

The various clays of Surrey have been the raw material for the manufacture of pottery since prehistory, and also for bricks and tiles since Roman times. Roof and hypocaust tiles were made during the Roman period at Ashtead, whilst beautiful medieval floor tiles were produced at Chertsey Abbey. Medieval pottery was manufactured in several places in west Surrey, and at Kingston, Cheam and also at Limpsfield on the east side of the county. The production of 'Surrey ware' con-

'Jumping a stone' in Shackstead Lane Bargate Stone Quarry, Godalming, in about 1920.

tinued into the 17th century, especially at Ash and other places straddling the border with Hampshire. Pottery production has continued at Wrecclesham to this day, where the pottery founded by Absalom Harris in 1873 became famous in the 1890s for 'Farnham Green-ware', which was developed using designs produced by the Farnham School of Art.

It was at Farnham in the last century that gravel was dug by physical labour from small pits along the Wey valley. Throughout the county, wherever there were patches of the stuff, small pits would be worked as and when the material was needed locally. But in recent years gravel extraction has been carried on in the county on a massive scale, using mechanical diggers and dredgers. The demand from road builders and contractors throughout Britain has seen the transformation of many parts of Thameside Surrey. Large areas of fertile farmland on the well-drained river gravels have been turned into vast lakes. This has proved a great boon to watersport enthusiasts, anglers and to aquatic wildlife, but has changed the character of villages like Thorpe for ever.

The chalk of the Downs has also been heavily quarried, as witnessed by the many large white scars visible on the south facing scarp from the Hog's Back in the west to Oxted in the east. The chalk was mainly used to produce lime for building-mortar and fertilizer. The largest chalk quarry in the county was at Betchworth, with a working face $\frac{1}{4}$ mile wide and 300 ft high. It is still a major landmark, visible for miles. Until 1960 this quarry had its own narrow gauge railway, where special wagons loaded with chalk were hauled to the kilns by steam engines. This was but one small task for an invention which had begun to change the face of Surrey over 100 years before.

15

THE AGE OF THE RAILWAY

The years following Napoleon's defeat at Waterloo in 1815 were punctuated with much unrest, prompted amongst other things by high prices for foodstuffs and the government's attempts to preserve the status quo. Whilst the pattern of wealth was changing, parliamentary 'democracy' was not, and the pressure for reform grew ever stronger in the late 1820s. This was also a period of technological development and invention, when many workers found their livelihood under threat from newly introduced machinery. Their anger was vent upon such labour saving inventions as threshing machines and in many places in England such machinery was smashed. Hayricks were set on fire, property ransacked and farmers and their families terrorised.

In 1830 matters came to a head, when gangs roamed the countryside threatening extortion and death to machine owners, who often received such threats in a letter signed by the enigmatic 'Captain Swing'. Mrs Langley living near Kingston received such a letter, although it was not signed by the 'Captain'. Postal historian James Grimwood-Taylor discovered the letter a few years ago and made a transcription of its scribbled contents. It began:

'Maddam Do Not be Surprised at this letter, for all your Nabours have Got the Same, or will Receive the Same, and Every one Reffusing the three Requests that are Demmanded will Suffer the same as the(y) have Suffered in . . . other Parts in Surrey that we Come threw, the first request are to Destroy yor Mashines. Second to give your men fifteen Shillings a week, third to send out ten Pounds By one of your Sevents . . .'

We do not know if Mrs Langley complied with these demands but perhaps, because there is no record surviving of damage to her property in Kingston, she did. In the rest of Surrey, riot and sometimes arson were reported at several places during these 'Swing Riots', including Molesey, Oxshott, Dorking and Woking. At Albury the village mill was destroyed and the culprit, a local labourer, was hanged for the crime. In nineteen other cases which came to court, eleven defendants were acquitted whilst eight received prison sentences. The riots had petered out by 1832 and Captain Swing, real or imaginary, was never heard of again.

By 1832 the forces of reform finally had their day and the first Act to remove the many abuses associated with Parliament was forced onto the statute book. Many 'pocket' boroughs lost their right to send MPs to Westminster and in Surrey the most infamous of these was Gatton. This 'rotten borough' had sent two burgesses to the House of Commons since about 1450, but for most of the time the total number of electors amounted to one man – the Lord of the Manor. In 1541, Sir Roger Copley, describing himself as 'Burgess and oonly Inhabitant' duly cast his vote and Gatton returned its 'freely chosen and elected' Members of Parliament.

The borough of Haslemere also lost its two MPs in 1832. This small town had been sending burgesses to Westminster since 1584 as strong supporters of Queen Elizabeth, especially when it came to voting her money, which is undoubtedly why she made Haslemere a parliamentary borough in the first place! Its most famous MP was James Oglethorpe, founder of the State of Georgia, who lived at Godalming. He had a nominal address in Haslemere in order to qualify but was hardly ever there, preferring London, Godalming, Cranham in Essex which he acquired through marriage, or Georgia, which is about as far as you could get in those days from the representation of your constituents in Haslemere!

Just six years after the first reform of Parliament, an invention which was to touch, then ultimately transform, the lives of almost every inhabitant rattled its way across the open Surrey countryside. The steam railway had arrived. It brought Surrey into London and the capital came out into Surrey. A blanket of brick eventually engulfed the northern part of the county, smothering ancient agricultural communities. Village after village was absorbed by streets of villa residences, new homes for those who could work each day in the city and then come home to the countryside their presence soon destroyed. In some parts of the county, the railway created entirely new towns, which sprouted in places once thinly populated.

Surrey could boast the first public railway in the world – the Surrey Iron Railway, which ran from Wandsworth to Croydon. The railway had a branch to Hackbridge on the river Wandle, which was later extended as the Croydon, Merstham & Godstone Iron Railway. The first section of line was officially opened on 26th July 1803, an event reported in *The*

Gatton 'Town Hall' where the election of the borough's two MPs took place until 1832.

European Magazine and London Review the following month. 'The Iron Railway from Wandsworth to Croydon was opened to the public for the conveyance of goods. The Committee went up in waggons drawn by one horse; and, to show how motion is facilitated by this ingenious and yet simple contrivance, a gentleman, with two companions, drove up the railway, in a machine of his own invention, without horses, at the rate of fifteen miles per hour.' This was no steam railway and the intended motive power was the horse – the 'simple contrivance' probably being something akin to a platelayer's hand-operated trolley. As reported, the railway was 'a conveyance for goods' and was not built to carry passengers.

In 1805 the line was continued to Merstham but that is as far as it ever reached. It had been the intention to construct a line all the way to Portsmouth, making it of great strategic value in the fight against Napoleon. However, after the decimation of the French fleet at Trafalgar, the British navy reigned supreme and support for the expensive iron railway collapsed. Forced to rely mainly on only local traffic, the railway was never a financial success. It could not compete

The London Necropolis near Woking had its own railway siding with private stations. Special trains brought coffins and mourners from Waterloo and decanted them as near to the graves as possible. Here a train steams into the cemetery's north station in about 1907.

against steam railways when they began their march across the county – the section to Merstham closed in 1839 and the remainder in 1846.

On 21st May 1838, the first steam-hauled train to carry fare paying passengers in Surrey rumbled into Woking Common station. It was the end of the line at the time and its passengers were decanted into some of the most barren and thinly populated countryside of Surrey. However, the first week of the line's existence proved auspicious, for it attracted about 10,000 customers, many of them racegoers bound for Epsom and the Derby. Woking Common, over a mile north-west of the moribund market town of Woking, was now but an hour from London.

The final destination of the railway was Southampton and the completed line was opened on 11th May 1840. Meanwhile, Woking Common had become a mecca for travellers throughout west Surrey who converged on the station by carriage, cart, horse or foot. There was little in the way of comforts for these earliest of commuters, nor anywhere for them to stable their horses whilst they were in London. Then a shrewd local business man, Edward Woods, opened The Railway Hotel and the new town of Woking had began. It was not long before the coaching trade on the nearby Portsmouth Turnpike dwindled and the inns along the route fell into decay.

The modern town of Woking has a curious and unique history. In spite of Edward Woods' enterprise there was no mad rush to build in the area, now just a short ride from the capital. It was not as the living that Londoners first came to Woking to stay, but as corpses in their thousands. On the heathlands near the station it was proposed to open a vast cemetery which would cater for all the dead of London. The population of the city was growing fast – it was just under one million at the time of the first census in 1801 with this figure reached two and a quarter million in 1851. With the birthrate rising dramatically, the death rate also substantially increased. The authorities were faced with a huge problem of where to bury all the dead, for they were very rapidly running out of burial space.

In the existing graveyards there were scenes of utter chaos. Graves were constantly being disturbed, dug up and reused and their previous contents left on the surface for the scavenging poor. A lucrative trade grew up in secondhand coffin furniture and firewood, whilst tons of human bones were gathered up to be crushed into fertilizer. The mass of decomposing corpses so near to habitation was being increasingly recognised as a health hazard by the medical authorities. They thought it poisoned the air but it certainly contaminated drinking water in adjacent wells. Matters came to a head in the great cholera epidemic of 1848–49, which claimed over 14,000 Londoners. An Act of Parliament was passed to allow the establishment of separate cemeteries away from the metropolis, but other government schemes to alleviate this massive problem came to naught.

It was at this point that Sir Richard Broun and Richard Sprye put forward their proposal for the establishment of the London Necropolis at Woking – a vast cemetery to cope with London's dead for ever. Essential to the scheme was the railway to carry the coffins and mourners to the grave and take the mourners home again. It was a business that could not fail to be highly profitable. Before Broun and Sprye could turn their idea into a commercial proposition, it was poached by another group of entrepreneurs, who formed the London Necropolis and National Mausoleum Company. Woking Common belonged to the Onslow family as Lords of the Manor and many villagers had commoners' rights upon the heath. It therefore needed an Act of Parliament to inclose the common and expunge those rights. This Bill duly received its Royal Assent on 30th June 1852, but not without opposition from some Surrey MPs. The MP for East Surrey, P.J. Locke King, raised no objection – he was a director of the Necroplis Company!

The necessary land, 2,328 acres of Woking Common, was purchased from the Onslows for £38,000. The commoners were bought off with £15,000. The Act specifically forbade the erection of any buildings on the site, other than those for cemetery purposes or staff accommodation. But it was not long before the company was drawing up a Bill to present to Parliament to allow them to sell off surplus land. Meanwhile 400 acres near Brookwood and furthest from Woking station were laid out for the cemetery, which opened on 7th November 1854 – the first burials being those of Mrs Store's still-born male twins, interred at the expense of her parish.

In 1855 Parliament gave permission for the selling of parts of the company's land around the station and Knaphill. It is clear from this Act that the establishment of a new town was envisaged, for it stipulated that five acres should be set aside for public buildings such as a church and a school. By 1869 the Necropolis Company had gained permission to sell for development all but 560 acres of their original purchase and the new town of Woking had begun its growth into Surrey's largest town. The original settlement of Woking, on the banks of the river Wey, was forced to adopt the prefix 'Old' to differentiate it from the new neighbour which had usurped its name.

The railway's march across Surrey was relentless. It reached Croydon in 1839 – the railway company bought the Croydon Canal, filled it in, and used much of its course for their line. Guildford was reached from Woking in 1845 and Godalming in 1849. Stations opened at Richmond in 1846, Epsom in 1847 and Chertsey in 1848. The good people of Kingston had disapproved of the railway in 1838, so it was routed via Surbiton. Very quickly afterwards a suburb of solid respectable villas grew up adjacent to the new Kingston station, as the station at Surbiton was first called.

Meanwhile, on the other side of the county, a second 'railway town' was beginning to sprout amongst once thinly populated damp green fields. Reigate had shunned the railway when a route to Brighton was proposed which would have passed close to the town. In the event, the railway went further east and spawned the town of Redhill. The railway to Brighton opened in 1841. From Redhill travellers could now reach London in just over the hour and from the capital be propelled right across Surrey into Sussex in a mere one hour and 17 minutes. In 1842 the railway at Redhill became a junction, when it was joined by the line from Tonbridge and in 1849 Redhill was linked to Reading via Farnborough, Guildford, Dorking and Reigate. By 1870 the new town of Redhill was well established, complete with all the facilities expected of a thriving Victorian town, including a market hall and several churches.

Innovation and change were not the sole prerogatives of the new towns of Redhill and Woking. In Guildford, Godalming and Reigate, for example, the railway brought newcomers and soon each place had its own share of suburban villas. Initially, the increase in population put the limited public services, such as water supply and sewerage, under serious

Rural Redhill before the coming of the railway.

pressure. In Godalming there was no mains water of any sort until 1880. Sewage disposal was limited to the occasional emptying of cesspits. These were often situated at the rear of premises, only a few feet from the well where water was obtained. As a result, the town suffered regular outbreaks of typhoid and even the dreaded cholera. The story was little different in nearby Guildford. In 1849 the author of a pamphlet written to draw attention to the dreadful state of the town's sewers described in detail 'the open mouth of a sewer disgorging its filth', which ran straight into the river Wey by the side of the Town Bridge. There were several outbreaks of cholera in Guildford, the last being in 1866. Eventually, between 1889 and 1895, the town was provided with what at the time was one of the most advanced sewerage systems in the world. At the same time an efficient method of rubbish collection was also introduced.

Guildfordians had had the benefit of gas street lighting as early as 1824, but it was left to the little town of Godalming to be the pioneer in the introduction of electricity. In 1881 the town council made the auspicious decision to abandon gas street lighting and change to electricity. The electricity was supplied by a generator driven by a waterwheel at the nearby leather mills at Westbrook. Later the generator was moved to White Hart Yard behind the High Street and driven by

An early view of Redhill.

a steam engine. The electricity was also available for supply to private homes and here was the great innovation. The equipment set up at Westbrook was in fact the world's first public power station and thus marked the birth of the electricity supply industry. Unfortunately, in those early days the system was not a great success and the town reverted to gas in 1884. However, a start had been made and once the equipment had been perfected, electric lighting began to oust gas from the streets of towns and cities throughout the world.

The church was the other light at the centre of any Victorian town or village in Surrey as, indeed, it was throughout England. From the late 17th century the Church of England had faced increasing competition for worshippers from the Nonconformists, especially following the Act of Toleration in 1689, which had allowed unmolested worship for religious groups such as Congregationalists. Baptists and Quakers. In the 18th century the Methodists were the driving force, led by John Wesley, who found England a more fertile preaching ground than Georgia, where he and his brother, Charles, had gone with James Oglethorpe in 1735. John Wesley rode the length and breadth of England preaching to all who would gather and listen, but it was in Surrey, at Leatherhead, that he preached his very last sermon in February 1791. A week later he was dead.

The Wesleys had brought a religious vitality into the lives of many ordinary folk, which seemed missing from the Church of England. But the Victorian period was to see a resurgence of zeal in the Established Church, one result of which was to have a lasting visual impact in so many of Surrey's towns and villages. The growing size of congregations, coupled with the desire to improve the status of the church within the community, led to a massive programme of church rebuilding and 'restoration' throughout the county. The result, as Ian Nairn wrote, was that 'the lightly restored churches of Surrey can be counted on the fingers and toes' but, as he continued, 'as the 19th century left Surrey richer in Gothic Revival churches than almost any other county, perhaps the result was worth it.'

Architecturally, the leader of this revival throughout England was Augustus Pugin. In Surrey, he tinkered with churches at Albury and Peper Harow but it was his pupil, Benjamin Ferrey, who made the first impact on the county's churches. Brockham church, built in 1846, is probably his most pleasing one, when viewed from across the picturesque village green. Some of the best Victorian churches in Surrey are by local architect Henry Woodyer, who was born in Guildford. His finest are undoubtedly at Buckland, built in 1860, at Hascombe, dating from 1864, and at Dorking, which was built four years later. Woodyer was also responsible for the church at York Town, where a thriving community had grown up on the infertile sandy heathland to serve the Royal Military Academy at nearby Sandhurst, over the border in Berkshire.

The Academy had been founded by Frederick, Duke of York, in 1812 – hence the name of the settlement. It marked the beginning of

The town of Godalming illuminated by electric light as depicted in *The Graphic* on 12th November 1881. Godalming was the first town in the world to have a public electricity supply service.

137

a permanent army presence in Surrey, which was to grow ever-stronger as the century progressed, especially following the establishment of barracks at Aldershot in the 1850s. Next door to York Town the Army Staff College was opened in 1862 and the villas, terraced houses and shops erected adjacent to it were named Cambridge Town after the then commander-in-chief, the Duke of Cambridge. Confusion with the famous university town, particularly in matters of postal deliveries, led to the name being changed to Camberley. Camps and barracks were built in many places in the county, particularly following the army reforms of the 1870s. These included Guildford, Deepcut, Pirbright, Blackdown and Caterham, where the Guards' Training Depot was transferred from Warley, Essex, in 1877.

The Royal Navy also had an important presence in Surrey during the first half of the 19th century. Before the invention of the electric telegraph, an ingenious method of rapid communication between the Admiralty in London and the fleet at Plymouth and Portsmouth was devised. A chain of towers was built across the country, each one visible by telescope to those either side of it. Messages were then passed down

This gun was placed on the green at Chobham in 1901 as a memorial to Queen Victoria who had reviewed the troops on nearby Chobham Common in 1853.

The royal tent and part of the great military camp on Chobham Common in 1853.

the line by semaphore. Several of these semaphore towers have survived in the county. The best is at Chatley Heath near Cobham, which has been restored and is now open to the public. It was in use between 1822 and 1847 and lies at the junction of the lines to Portsmouth and Plymouth.

In 1853, as war with Russia threatened, it was decided to hold a great military camp on Chobham Common, as a show of strength. On 14th June nearly 10,000 troops gathered on the common, where they took part in various military manoeuvres, including a mock battle, at a camp which lasted until 25th August. The highlight of the proceedings was the visit of Queen Victoria accompanied by Prince Albert, who reviewed the troops on 21st June, watched by a crowd estimated to be 100,000 strong. Details of the event were recalled in the Chobham parish magazine of March 1901, in memory of the recently dead queen. The magazine reported that 'Waterloo was besieged, 14,000 tickets were issued for Chertsey in three hours, and when all the "specials" had left the station the platforms still swarmed with eager passengers, many being ladies dressed in riding habits. From 300 to 400 horse-boxes were despatched.'

At Chertsey, demand for horse-drawn transport to Chobham was so great that only those who could afford the charge of up to £1 got a ride. Many thousands walked whilst Chobham experienced its first traffic jam.

The queen and her party travelled down from Nine Elms to Staines, from where she was driven in an open carriage to the camp. 'Punctually at 11 o'clock the Royal Standard was hoisted, and announced to the waiting thousands the queen's arrival. To the delight of all, she alighted and mounted a dark bay horse with rich gold trappings, she wore a dark blue riding habit with basque jacket setting close to her figure, having on her breast a rich gold aiguilette and brilliant garter star, on her head a round riding hat with a military plume of red and white feathers in front.'

The Times reported: 'It is quite impossible to exaggerate the brilliancy of the scene as the Royal procession at a slow pace passed from regiment to regiment, each drawn up on its respective parade ground, the band of each saluting with the National Anthem and presenting arms. The splendour and extent of the cortège was a thing of itself worth going some distance to see.' After the inspection the Royal party watched a sham fight and then came the 'finest feature of the day's proceedings', as all 10,000 troops paraded past the queen. Finally Queen Victoria and her party took lunch in a large marquee before returning by carriage to Staines station.

Once the queen had departed it began to pour with rain, bringing a stampede of spectators along the road to Chertsey where, as the Chobham parish magazine reported, 'the station was a scene of wild confusion, and night descended before the enormous traffic could be overtaken.' In this way there came to an end Surrey's most spectacular military event in peacetime, its splendour soon to be marred by disease and death upon the stark battlefields of the Crimea.

16

THE PLAYGROUND OF LONDON

By the end of Queen Victoria's reign almost every corner of Surrey was within easy reach of London. Not only was the populace of the city on the move into the Surrey countryside, but also many of its institutions such as orphanages, hospitals and lunatic asylums as well. A number of asylums in particular were built in the Epsom and Banstead area. Many schools also moved to Surrey or were founded in the county during Queen Victoria's reign. For example, Epsom College was opened by Prince Albert in 1855 as the 'Royal Medical Benevolent College', principally for the sons of medical men. St John's School for the sons of clergymen was founded in 1852 and moved to Leatherhead 20 years later, whilst the famous Charterhouse also removed itself from the smog of London to Godalming in 1872.

Many writers, artists, and men and women of commerce found a retreat amongst the hills and heaths of the county. The scientist and mountaineer, Professor John Tyndall, discovered Hindhead as an English substitute for his beloved Alps. He was soon extolling the health giving properties of the clean air of the Surrey 'mountains' and others followed him there. Sir Arthur Conan Doyle had temporarily moved to Switzerland for the health of his first wife, who suffered from TB. Upon hearing of Tyndall's discovery of Hindhead 'ozone', he arranged for a house, Undershaw, to be built there. Although his wife was not cured, Conan Doyle always claimed that she had gained several more precious years of life as a consequence of their move to Hindhead. George Bernard Shaw came to nearby Woolmer Hill on his honeymoon in 1898. Apparently, he did not particularly enjoy the experience and ended up with a broken leg. Later, he rented a house at Hindhead called 'Blen-Cathra' but he soon got bored with life in the country and returned to London.

Many other writers who were famous in their day but are now almost forgotten also took up residence at Hindhead. These included the Canadian, Grant Allen, who in 1895 wrote a controversial book about social and sexual problems called *The Woman Who Did*. Indeed, at one time there were so many writers and thinkers at Hindhead that one wag nicknamed it 'Mindhead'. Tyndall was appalled by this invasion of his precious 'English Switzerland'. He built a huge artificial screen, disguised as a clump of trees, to hide the other houses that had destroyed his view.

Many more in the county were to suffer as Tyndall had. The tide of building which followed the railway began to engulf thousands of acres of farmland and market gardens. By 1900 ribbons of houses had reached the foot of the Downs in a number of places. Historian, Dorothy L. Powell wrote of Caterham at this time, 'the whole of the valley and the slopes on either side are now full of houses of various sizes, from small estates to cottages. Only south of the old village, on the highest part of the chalk . . . the parish is distinctly rural still.'

Some writers appeared to welcome this smothering of the countryside, such as a certain Arthur Henry Anderson who commented that 'human beings are more important than scenery, and if it came to a choice between no houses and ugly houses, I should plump for the houses . . .

Empire Day at Woking in 1908. Wholesale redevelopment in recent years has made this view unrecognisable.

A rural scene in Linkfield Lane, Redhill, in 1906.

even at the cost of ugliness.' This view was not shared by a famous resident of Epsom, Lord Rosebery, who, when asked to write the introduction to a guide of Epsom began starkly: 'I am desired to write a few words of preface . . . And, when one comes to think of it, one must write it soon, for there will soon be little material for a preface or guide. When I first came to live in Epsom . . . it was a sleepy town, surrounded by long stretches of down and common. Its perennial slumber was broken twice a year by race meetings. . . . Now all that is changed . . . the builder . . . has come and cut into the lanes and hedges. A gaunt asylum shrouds the misery of hundreds or thousands of the mad patients of London. One or two commons are enclosed. The stray edges of greenery, which were the heritage of the wayfarer, are gradually being fenced in . . . The new Epsom is only a fragment of the past, and only a fragment of the future.'

A large fragment of that past and future was, of course, the racing on Epsom Downs, 'when the followers and camp followers of the Turf stormed the neighbourhood during a few agitated days, then struck

Durbar wins the 1914 Derby.

their tents and left the town, sodden and exhausted'. Increasingly, in the Victorian period much more of Surrey became the playground of London, just as Epsom had been since the day when the Derby was first run in 1780. This flat race for three year old colts and fillies was named after Lord Derby, whilst the course's other famous race, the Oaks, first run in 1779, acquired its name from Lord Derby's house near Carshalton.

Surrey had several other famous racecourses to challenge Epsom in the early days. Racing started at Egham in 1734 and it was a popular meeting often attended by royalty, particularly William IV. The course was actually just outside the town at Runnymede. There were races at Reigate, Croydon and Guildford, where huge crowds would gather on Merrow Downs. All these courses were open meetings. As the 19th century progressed they attracted an increasing number of unruly characters, who used the races as an excuse for robbery and riot. As a result, in 1875, the first enclosed park course in Britain was opened at Sandown near Esher. Sandown was much patronised by the Prince of Wales, later Edward VII, and its most famous races are the Eclipse Stakes on the flat and the Whitbread Gold Cup over the jumps. Nearby at Molesey, Hurst Park opened in the 1880s on the site of the open Hampton racecourse. It closed in 1962 and a housing estate now occupies the site. After Hurst Park came Kempton Park, then in

144

Middlesex, opened in 1889 and now famous for the King George VI Steeplechase run on Boxing Day. Lingfield Park was opened in 1890 and now boasts, in addition to the turf course, an 'all weather' track, which enables flat races to take place even in the middle of winter.

A prerequisite of the success of these park courses was that they were all within easy distance of a railway station, and therefore a short train ride for Londoners. Being enclosed courses, the 'calibre' of the racegoers could be controlled at the gates and the end of most open courses soon followed. Guildford and Reigate races had already ceased but those at Egham survived until 1884. Here large gangs would routinely descend upon the crowd, robbing and assaulting racegoers at will, with the police almost powerless to intervene. Matters reached a head after the races of 1884 when the police refused to attend any further meetings. It was the end of the Egham Races.

Croydon Races transferred to a park course at Gatwick, now in West Sussex, in 1891. Gatwick was a popular course, especially for jump racing – under wartime conditions the Grand National was run here from 1916 to 1918. Gatwick developed a small aerodrome in the middle of the course which was eventually to spell the end of its racing! Thus, by 1900, only Epsom continued as a mainly open course, reliant on that national institution, the Derby, for its survival. Today, although television has

The Royal train carrying King Edward VII to Epsom Downs station on Derby Day in 1908.

Reigate Races,

FIRST DAY;—WEDNESDAY, 25th MAY, 1836;

FIRST RACE.

SWEEPSTAKES of 20 sov. each; h. ft.; for two yrs. old. Colts, 8st. 6lb.; fillies 8st 3lb. Three quarters of a mile. Winners before running for this Stake to carry 4lb extra; if twice 7lb. Start at Half-past One.

Sir G. Heathcote's ch. f. Countess, by The Colonel out of Jane, by Moses Crimson, grey cap Buckle 1

Mr. Harrisonia gr. c. by Albany out of Agnes, by President ......

Mr. Farrell's br. c. by The Colonel, out of Pinious Yellow, black cap Farrell . 2

SECOND RACE.

A GOLD CUP, value 150 gs. given and won by David Robertson, Esq. in 1835, at regiven for 1836, added to a Sweepstakes of 10 sov. each; about two Miles and a Half The winner to be sold for 500 sov. if demanded in the usual way. Three yrs. old, 7st 7lb.; four, 8st. 6lb.; five, 9st. 2lb.; and aged, 9st 6lb. Mares and Geldings allowed 3lb. The winner of the Epsom Cup to carry 5lb. extra. The winner of the Cup to pay towards the Improvements of the Course, £10. At Two.

Sir G. Heathcote's Quadroon ...... Crimson, grey cap F. Buckle

Mr. Robertson's Lucifer ...... Pink and black stripe, cap the same Twitchett

Mr. Crommelin's b. m. Zittella, 5 yrs. ......

Mr. Sowerby's b. f. Bodice, 4 yrs. ...... Light blue jacket and cap 4

Mr. Dawson's b. h. Morpeth, 5 yrs. ...... Yellow, black cap

Mr. Batchin's br. m. Levity, 5 yrs. ...... Blue, white cap Balchin 5

Mr. T. Bainbridge's br. g. Speculation, aged ...... Blue, black cap

Mr. Gardner's ch. c. Idiot, 4 yrs. ...... White, blue sleeves, white cap

Duke of Richmond's Elizander, 4 yrs. ...... Yellow, red cap, gold tassel

Duke of Richmond's Pussey, 5 yrs. ...... same 3

Mr. Theobald's ch. n. Olympic ...... Pink and black stripe, cap same Macdonald 2

Col. Peel's ch. c. Jacob Faithful, 3 yrs. ...... Purple, orange cap Pavis 1

THIRD RACE.

A PLATE of 50 sov. given by the Ladies of Surrey, for Horses which have never won before the day of entry. Three yrs. old, 7st. 7lb.; four, 8st. 5lb.; five, 9st.; six and aged, 9st. 2lb. Mares and Geldings allowed 3lb. Heats: about a mile and half. The winner to be sold for 120 sov. Entrance, 2 sov. to go towards the improvements of the Course. At Half past Two.

Count Bethany's ch. f. The Sylphide, by Tiresias out of the Fairy Queen, 5 yrs. ...... Yellow, blue sleeves, black cap S. Day 1 | 2

Mr. W. Edwards' ch. c. Hatfield, 3 yrs. ...... White, blue cap Flatman 2 | 1

Mr. Price's ch. g. by Aaron, 3 yrs. ...... Red, black cap Tiny 3

Mr. Molineux's g. f. by Dunisnane, dam by Muley, 3 yrs. Brown, purple and white sleeves, cap same 3

FOURTH RACE.

THE HUNTERS' GOLD CUP, value 100 sov. 50 sov. being given by the Reigate Racing Committee, and increased by a Sweepstakes of 5 sov. each; the rest in specie; or Hunters which have been regularly hunted this season, with any established Pack of Fox-Hounds, or belonging to Subscribers to the Royal Surrey Stag-Hounds, and which have been regularly hunted with them this season. 12st. each. Winners before running, to carry 7lb. extra; if twice 10lb. Thorough bred Horses to carry 10lb. extra. Heats: about two miles. The winner to be sold for 120 sov. if demanded in the usual way. The winner to pay towards the Improvements of the Course, £5. At Half past Three.

Mr. Thompson's b. m. Agnes, by Robin Hood, aged, Black, orange cap 3

Mr. Knight's ch. g. Gameboy by Regalia, 5 yrs. ...... Black, white cap 2

Mr. Robertson's b. g. Rupert Pink and bk. stripe, cap same Macdonald

Mr. J. Matthews' ch. g. Ace of Diamonds, aged, Green body, pink sl. green cap Buckle

Mr. Agate's b. h. Nonesuch, 4 yrs. ...... Blue, black cap Balchin 3

Mr. G. Pannel's b. h. Hokee Pokey, aged Blue, yel. sl. wh. cap Owner 5 | 6

Mr. Baring's b. g. Lofty, aged, ... White, black cap Capt. Beecher 3 | 4

Mr. T. Bainbridge's br. g. Stradbally, 5 yrs. Blue, black cap, Dakeray 2

THE RACE DINNER will take place on the First Day, immediately after the races, at the SWAN INN, Reigate.

JOHN HARMAN, Esq.
CHARLES H. TURNER, Jun. Esq. } Stewards.

J. FARRELL, EPSOM, CLERK OF THE COURSE.

Printed by W. Allingham, Reigate.

The racecard for the Reigate Races in 1836.

contributed to a decline in racegoers, who once blanketed the Downs in their tens of thousands, the Derby is still the most important flat race in Britain.

Many other sports played a part in Surrey life down the years, none more so than cricket. The county can claim the first known reference to the game. It occurs in a document of 1598 relating to a dispute over a piece of land, which refers to events at least 50 years before: 'John Derrick, gent, one of the Queen's Majestie's coroners of the county of Surrey, aged fifty-nine, saith this land before mentioned lett to John Parvish, inn holder, deceased, that he knew it for fifty years or more. It lay waste, and was used and occupied by the inhabitants of Guildford . . . When he was a scholler in the Free School of Guildford, he and several of his fellows did run and play there at crickett and other plaies.' This was not of course quite the game as it later evolved, but the tradition of cricket in Surrey surely stems from that time.

Surrey County Cricket Club was founded in 1845 and has had numerous famous players who made their mark on the game over the years. Fine players, too numerous to mention more than a few – William Caffyn of Reigate and Henry Jupp of Dorking in the early days, Surridge, Fender, Bedser, May, Laker, Lock and Barrington in this century – all were players of the highest calibre. Then there was the enigmatic Julius Caesar of Godalming, who joined the Surrey club in 1849. Caesar was chosen for the first England team to tour abroad

Leith Hill in 1890. A mecca for walkers and cyclists.

which, remarkably, went to Canada and the USA, where it was unbeaten even when playing against teams of 22 men. In 1863–64 he was in the team which toured Australia and again returned home unbeaten. Unfortunately, his life was dogged by misfortune – he accidently shot dead a beater whilst on a pheasant shoot near his home. The tragedy profoundly affected his game and he retired soon after. In 1872 he became cricket coach to Charterhouse School but two years later his wife died and in 1876 his eldest son committed suicide. These two further tragedies pushed Julius Caesar down the slippery slope to alcoholism, which eventually killed him. It was a sad end for such a brilliant and well respected Surrey cricketer. But Julius would have been pleased to know that his game still thrives today on numerous, and often still rural, cricket greens the length and breadth of his county.

Although the present administrative county of Surrey cannot boast a football league team, two highly successful teams, Wimbledon and Crystal Palace share a ground at Selhurst Park in the London Borough

The delights of the bicycle before the First World War. Mr T. H. L. Grosvenor sets out from Redhill on a moth hunting expedition.

of Croydon. Wimbledon's rise from non-league status to victory over Liverpool in the FA Cup Final of 1988 is legendary. They were not, however, the first Surrey team to win the cup – a team of ex-Charterhouse pupils, the Old Carthusians, won it in 1881, the last amateur team to do so. Many have hopes that Woking may soon follow the same path as Wimbledon. Woking FC was founded in 1889 and the club includes the FA Amateur Cup of 1958 amongst its successes. Most recently Woking are remembered for their FA Cup run in the 1990/91 season, which included a 4-2 defeat of West Bromwich Albion, and the crowning glory of their 1993/94 season – victory over Runcorn in the FA Trophy final at Wembley.

Several Surrey towns, including Kingston and Dorking, were renowed for the traditional mass game of Shrove Tuesday football. At Dorking the

The old and the new – W. A. Scantlebury's removal vans in the 1920s at Woking.

teams consisted of 'Eastenders' and 'Westenders', depending on which end of the town a 'player' came from. On the day of the game, many people were up early, especially the shopkeepers – there would be no trade for them today and the morning was spent boarding up the windows of their shops. Only the pubs would do well on this particular Tuesday. A band then appeared, marching slowly along the High Street, its members strangely dressed, a cacophony of noise coming from whistles, pipes, triangles and drums. This was the 'Taffer Bolts Band'. At the front of the march came a man carrying a cross from which were suspended three coloured footballs – a blue and white one, a larger one painted gold, the other red and green. Some followers of the band carried a collection box to raise money to pay for the inevitable broken windows and other damage which was to come.

At 2 o'clock in the afternoon, play commenced with the town crier or a leading inhabitant kicking off with the red and green ball at the gates of St Martin's church. There was no limit to the size of the teams and often spectators and players seemed indivisible. The object of the game was to retain the ball in your own half of the town, but this seemed immaterial to most of the players. Throughout the afternoon the battle for the ball raged up and down the street. Then at 6 o'clock, with one last shout, the

Golf on Reigate Heath in 1913.

game came to an end, the players and most of the spectators retiring to the nearest pub.

Unfortunately for exponents and fans of this annual riot, during the 1890s there were a rising number of objections. Some shopkeepers complained about the damage and the loss of trade, whilst Surrey County Council claimed the game illegal, as an obstruction to the highway. The local Dorking Urban District Council were in favour of continuing the tradition, but in 1897 the County Council drafted in extra police and posted notices banning the game. However, a large crowd still assembled on Shrove Tuesday and a local councillor, John Maybank, did the honours at the kick off. The police now joined the players in the scrummage for the football, but to confuse them a number of footballs appeared to be in play at the same time. By the end of the match the constables had captured eight of them and also arrested 52 players! Each of those arrested was fined a shilling with four shillings costs by the local magistrates, for being in breach of the Highways Act of 1835. In 1898 the ban was broken again and there were 60 arrests, but the crowds attending were noticeably smaller. The decline was rapid from then on, until in 1907 not one brave soul turned up at 2 o'clock on Shrove Tuesday to carry on the game.

Many other sports have proved an attraction to both Surrey inhabitants and Londoners seeking relaxation. The county has always been well provided with a number of excellent golf courses, particularly Walton Heath, where the British Open has been played. Unfortunately, such is the popularity of the game today that the rash of recently built courses poses a real threat to the character of the Surrey countryside. Lawn tennis is one of a large number of games invented during the Victorian period. Surrey provides the headquarters of the All England Croquet and Lawn Tennis Club at Wimbledon, where the best in the world gather each year to play in the oldest and most prestigious tournament on the international circuit.

For many middle class Londoners and suburban dwellers at the turn of the century the highlight of their leisure time was a boat trip or scull upon the Thames or Wey. In the summer the queues for Molesey Lock often reached M25 traffic jam proportions. Many more took the train into the still rich countryside of Surrey for a day's rambling, aided by the plethora of guide books published to cover every nook and cranny of the county. This movement was particularly inspired by the writings of the likes of 'Walker Miles' and Anthony Collett. Armed with their books, ramblers entered Surrey with a pioneering spirit akin to that of an African explorer – the goal might be Victoria Falls or simply the top of Leith Hill. It was clearly the first stage in the colonisation of a backward country. One guidebook entitled *Country Rambles round London* majestically proclaimed: 'By great good fortune the world's vastest city is within an hour's journey of some of its most beautiful scenery. Business travellers carry the seeds of London with them; wherever they plant their feet, a new suburb springs beneath them, like the daisy – "the white man's footstep" – which followed the caravans across the American plains.' But there were still undiscovered places to explore down 'green paths . . . secretly threading the quieter fields like a hare's trail across a village hillside.' Those who sought the Surrey countryside at weekends often ended up as Surrey inhabitants.

The 1880s saw the invention of the safety bicycle, which quickly replaced the cumbersome and often dangerous 'ordinary' or penny-farthing. Now not even the train was needed to take the smog-choked city dweller deep into Surrey. The county became the mecca for the capital's thousands of cycling enthusiasts heading down the Portsmouth road to Ripley or beyond. The Devil's Punchbowl at Hindhead or Box Hill were favourite Surrey targets for the intrepid rider. Many of the

151

county's inns, hotels and cafés catered especially for those who had found the new freedom of the open road. It was not to last, for upon the horizon there came a drone like a bee. By the mid-1900s the cyclist was often forced to watch this destroyer of the peaceful scene from the depths of a roadside ditch, and Kenneth Grahame's description of its coming must have seemed singularly appropriate: 'It was on them! The "poop-poop" rang with a brazen shout in their ears, they had a moment's glimpse of an interior of glittering plate-glass and rich morocco, and the magnificent motor-car, immense, breath-snatching, passionate, with its pilot tense and hugging his wheel, possessed all earth and air for the fraction of a second, flung an enveloping cloud of dust that blinded and enwrapped them utterly, and then dwindled to a speck in the far distance . . ' Another major player upon the stage of change had arrived in Surrey.

17

IN PEACE AND WAR

The county of Surrey has played a surprisingly important role in the development of the motor-car. A Farnham man, John Henry Knight, is credited with building the first British car in 1895. The county has been the birthplace of a large number of different makes of vehicle propelled by the internal combustion engine – at Farnham it was the 'Pilgrim' motor-car, at Egham they built Lagondas and even Godalming had its 'Victoria' model.

At Guildford, John and Raymond Dennis set up their business, making and selling bicycles, in 1895. By 1898 they were manufacturing motorised tricycles which could ascend the bumps of Guildford High Street at the then breath-taking speed of 16 mph. It was not long before the brothers very successfully turned their attention to the production of four-wheelers. By 1900, business had expanded so much that they began the construction of a factory in Onslow Street, Guildford. This building is still standing today and has claims to be the oldest surviving purpose-built car factory in the world. However, by 1905, with business still growing rapidly, the Dennis brothers began a second factory at Woodbridge. Later the firm ceased the production of cars and turned its attention to the manufacture of the commercial vehicles for which it became so famous. These included buses, lorries, dustcarts and fire engines.

The motor-car was not well received by the Surrey authorities, who attempted to limit its speed on the open road to 20 mph. In towns the limit was half that and many Surrey magistrates soon gained a reputation for the swingeing fines they imposed upon those who dared to use the full power of their motors. Some Surrey towns were infamous amongst the motoring fraternity for the efficiency of their speed traps. The newly formed Automobile Association, whose staff traversed the roads by bicycle, often stationed themselves at the entrance to towns like Godalming and Reigate to warn their members when a trap was in operation! These restrictions were damaging to motor manufacturers seeking somewhere to test their products. There were no such restrictions in operation on the Continent and British car makers were obviously at a disadvantage.

All this was to change, thanks to the foresight of one Surrey man – Hugh Locke King. He lived in a large house near Weybridge station on the edge of St George's Hill and for generations his family had been major landowners in the area. Locke King was a confirmed car enthusiast and he was particularly concerned that British car makers should be given every facility to develop vehicles as good as their counterparts in Europe. He recognised that Britain needed a purpose-built track on private land, where cars could be tested and raced flat out without their drivers facing arrest and heavy fines.

Below St George's Hill, the Locke King estate included a large tract of damp and marshy meadowland astride the meandering river Wey. Locke King was determined that this was the spot where his motor track should be built. In 1906 plans were drawn up, and in a mere eight months the meadowland was transformed. It was a colossal undertaking which employed 2,000 men working almost non-stop. The river was diverted and bridged in two places; massive concrete banking nearly 30 ft high was constructed on the bends and 350,000 cubic yards of soil and sand excavated.

The new track was named Brooklands and the motor course was officially opened on 17th June 1907. It was the first in the world. In just a few short months peaceful meadows had been turned into $2^3/_4$ miles of oval, 100 ft wide concrete track, with a separate finishing straight in the middle. The first race meeting was held on 6th July 1907.

Motor racing at Brooklands in the 1930s.

The excitement of the open road at Caterham in the 1920s. The motorcycle is an American 'Harley Davidson', the car an English 'Humber'.

The competing cars carried no numbers and spectators were expected to identify them by means of the racing colours worn by the drivers, rather like jockeys. This similarity with horse racing extended to the entry fees and prize money, which were in sovereigns, whilst the results of each race were put up on a board, just like those still seen today just a few miles down the road at Sandown. It was no coincidence that the starter at this first meeting just happened to be a member of the Jockey Club! Modern motor racing circuits still have a paddock but the original was at Brooklands.

Once the teething problems had been ironed out, Brooklands became an extremely popular track not only for cars but also for motorbikes and cycles.

In the same year that motor racing commenced at Brooklands, a certain Alliott Verdon-Roe arrived there to experiment with that new wondrous invention, the heavier than air flying machine, first flown by the Wright brothers in 1903. In the early morning of a fine day in September 1907 the intrepid Verdon-Roe succeeded in launching his newly built machine off the embankment of the motor track and he glided a distance of 79 ft, just 10 ft off the ground. Verdon-Roe's exploit was not officially witnessed and, like the successful powered flights he made the following June, did not go down in the record books as the first in Britain. The company that Verdon-Roe founded was called Avro and was to become famous for many successful aircraft over the years. However, the official honour of the first flight in Britain went to an American, Colonel Samuel Cody, who successfully flew for just over ¼ mile at Farnborough, just over the border in Hampshire, on 16th October 1908.

It was not long before Brooklands developed as the pioneering centre of aviation in Britain and many famous names flew here, including Tommy Sopwith, Harry Hawker and John Alcock. Alcock learnt to fly at Brooklands and was trained by Mrs Hilda B. Hewlett, wife of the then popular novelist, Maurice Hewlett. In August 1911 Hilda Hewlett had became the first woman to be granted a pilot's certificate. Alcock went on to become the legendary aviator who, with Arthur Whitten Brown, was the first to fly the Atlantic in 1919.

The aircraft in which Alcock and Brown so bravely crossed that vast ocean was a Vickers Vimy. It was built by Vickers at their aircraft factory, which had been established at Brooklands in 1915. Many famous aircraft were to emerge from this factory over the years, including the Wellington bomber, which played an important part in the victory over the Germans in the Second World War, especially during the early part of the war. The frame of the Wellington was designed by Barnes Wallis who carried out many of his researches at Brooklands. It was here that he designed the famous 'Dambusters' bouncing bomb which was used to attack the Mohne and Ruhr dams in Germany in May 1943.

The potential of the aircraft in wartime had been recognised during the First World War. This was a conflict where, for the first time, some of those left by the firesides at home became directly involved. The threat did not, however, come from German aircraft, whose range at the time was far too short. In 1915 the Germans really brought the war to England, when the long shadow of the Zeppelin airship was cast across the towns and villages of England and German bombs brought death to places like Lowestoft. On the 13th October 1915 a Zeppelin appeared over Surrey and flew towards Guildford, where it dropped several bombs. If the target was the town, the Germans missed and some of the bombs came down at St Catherines where they claimed their only Surrey victim – a swan paddling innocently along the river Wey.

The First World War brought massive army activity to Surrey, not only at the existing barracks, but also at huge temporary camps set up, for example, at Witley and Woodcote. At Witley, as at most of these places, local tradesmen benefited from the thousands of extra customers, including troops from Canada. Shops built of galvanised iron and wood

Preparing for war – a machine gun detachment of the 4th Battalion of the Queen's Regiment training at Lingfield in 1913.

Army Camp on Coulsdon Common in about 1915.

German POWs marching to the prison camp at Frith Hill, Frimley, during the First World War.

sprang up along the Portsmouth road, which passed through the camp, and this commercial settlement, with cafés and a cinema as well, became known as 'Tin Town'. These camps were the slickly operated factories for the cannon fodder of the Western Front, where thousands of Surrey men were included amongst the dead.

The end of the First World War came in November 1918 when the enemy was finally hammered into submission, but a more deadly foe was already stalking the homes of Britain. The Spanish flu, nicknamed 'the plague of the Spanish lady', was to claim more lives throughout Europe than had perished in the fighting. The epidemic was at its worst during the autumn of 1918 and into early 1919 and many of Surrey's schools were closed for the duration.

Following the victory, the giant 'war machine' took a long time to run down and many Canadian troops stationed in Surrey spent a frustrating time waiting to go home. Matters came to a head in June 1919 when the Canadians at Witley rioted and burnt down 'Tin Town'. At Epsom they wrecked the local police station and, it is said, killed a policeman, although that matter seems to be missing from the records.

This 'war to end all wars' left every community in Britain bereft of so many of its menfolk. Every part of Surrey felt the loss and today we have those long lists of names upon too many memorials to remind us of that tragic waste of life.

Several of the those war memorials were designed by Surrey's most famous architect, Edwin Lutyens, including those at Abinger and Busbridge, near Godalming. Lutyens was also responsible for the nation's principal memorial, the Cenotaph in Whitehall. He was born in London in 1869 but much of his early life was spent at Thursley. He is best remembered for his fine country houses, built mainly around the turn of the century. In many cases the gardens of these houses were laid out to designs by Gertude Jekyll, the talented gardener, embroiderer, artist and photographer.

Gertrude Jekyll was also the author of numerous books, mainly on gardening, but including *Old West Surrey* published in 1904. In this book Gertrude Jekyll faithfully recorded all she could about the rapidly vanishing way of life in this rural corner of the county. It was a book many years ahead of its time and included the significant plea, 'Even from the point of view of commercial convenience and well-being it would be well if there could be some strict censorship exercised in the matter of the removal or rebuilding of houses in such conspicuous positions as the streets of country towns.' It was a plea which went unnoticed throughout much of Surrey until the introduction of town conservation areas in the 1970s.

Meanwhile, some steps were being taken to prevent the wholesale destruction of the Surrey countryside, and these were spearheaded by the work of the National Trust. A major victory for preservation was

A solid tyred 'East Surrey' omnibus at Felbridge.

'Pilgrims' celebrate the dedication of Colley Hill near Reigate for public recreation in 1913.

won when Leopold Salomons of Norbury Park, Mickleham, presented the summit of Box Hill to the National Trust in 1914. Colley Hill above Reigate had been saved two years before, thanks to an appeal run by *The Spectator* to raise money for its purchase. Thus the Downs became a bulwark against the invasion of bricks and mortar, a defence now bolstered by post-Second World War planning laws and the 'green belt' policy.

By the 1920s the spread of London had reached as far as Merton, but from there the land to the south was still predominantly rural. Then, in 1926, the Northern Line of the Underground reached Morden. At first, the steps of this terminus led out into a world of green fields and hedgerows, where small streams like the Beverley Brook and the Hogsmill meandered, crossed by country lanes at shallow fords, or watersplashes as they were known. Adjacent to Morden Park with its Georgian mansion, small weather-boarded cottages were scattered along the edge of Lower Morden Green, where the lane led past Peacock Farm and Hatfield Farm. The scene was now to change – replaced by streets of semi-detached and terraced mock Tudor houses with names like Aragon Road, Cardinal Avenue and Cranmer Close.

From Morden through Malden to Kingston and down to Ewell, Epsom, Cheam and Sutton there came this extraordinary outburst of home building. Britain was becoming a nation of home owners and many of them wanted to live in Surrey. Newspapers, magazines and guidebooks bulged with advertisements extolling the delights of this or that suburb and happiness was yours for a £25 deposit.

At weekends those from the suburbs came out in their Morris Eights, Austin Sevens and Ford Eights and Surrey began to experience serious traffic problems. The first jams had begun back in the early 1920s on the Portsmouth road through Kingston. The solution was a new road, opened in 1926, which cut across the countryside to the east of the town. It was Britain's first traffic bypass. Similar roads were constructed in the 1930s to avoid Guildford, Godalming, Mickleham and Caterham among others. A road across open commons was built as a link to the new Hampton Court Bridge, designed by Lutyens. A seemingly unstoppable process had begun which continues to eat away at the Surrey countryside to this day.

In the inter-war period Surrey not only had an important role in aircraft manufacture but, at Croydon, a public airport, which opened in March 1920, was developed. Croydon Airport is best remembered for the part it played in the pioneering exploits of early long distance aviators, including Amy Johnson. In May 1930 she flew a de Havilland

A typical housing advertisement of the 1930s.

Building the Caterham bypass in 1937.

Moth biplane solo from Croydon to Darwin in Australia. The journey, which, of course, required regular refuelling stops, took three weeks to complete. In December 1932 she flew from Cape Town to Croydon in a week. An interesting flight took place in April 1937 when two Japanese airmen, Masaaki Iinuma and Kenjii Tsukagoshi, landed at Croydon, having taken just under four days to fly from Tokyo.

By 1938 Croydon Airport was proving to be too small for the rapidly increasing number of civil flights and British Airways (a different airline from the modern BA) transferred their day flights to Gatwick. But, along with several other airfields in Surrey, Croydon still had an important role to play in the events which followed the declaration of war in September 1939.

In the spring and summer of 1940 the threat of invasion was very real. On the evening of 14th May the Secretary of State for War, Anthony Eden, broadcast to the nation. He called for ex-servicemen and those exempt from military service to take up arms in defence of their threatened country. Many hundreds of Surrey men queued outside their local police stations the following day to sign up for service in the Local Defence Volunteers, soon to be known as the Home Guard. Surrey had no shortage of resident ex-army officers to lead these volunteers. Typical of them was Colonel G.C. Hodgson, who

162

was appointed commanding officer of what later became the 53rd Surrey Battalion of the Home Guard. Hodgson had joined the Indian Army in 1897 and was severely wounded during the Younghusband Expedition, which had fought its way through Tibet to Lhasa in 1904. As a result he had been awarded the DSO. The men of Hodgson's Home Guard covered the Dittons, Molesey and Esher areas and their responsibilities included guarding Hampton Court Bridge.

The dangers of 1940 also prompted the construction of a chain defences along the North Downs and in the river valleys. This 'GHQ Stopline' consisted of anti-tank ditches, anti-tank concrete 'pimples' and a variety of different types of pillboxes, strategically placed. Many of these defences can still be seen today and are now receiving much warranted interest from military historians and archaeologists. It was only by luck and courage that these defences were never used and that the Home Guard were never called to fight in earnest. After the war it was discovered that one of the German invasion plans involved landing a large force on the Sussex coast, with the initial spearhead then driving north for the Guildford gap, in a movement to outflank the defenders of London. Had the invasion ever come about, Surrey towns and villages like Godalming, Bramley and Shalford might have given their names to crucial battles of the Second World War.

This did not happen, because of those brave 'few' who risked, and often gave, their lives over the fields of southern England in that warm late summer of 1940. On 15th August German aircraft attacked Croydon

Croydon Airport in the 1930s.

aerodrome. However, most of their bombs fell on factories on the fringes of the target but 63 people, mostly civilians, were killed. The squadron of Hawker Hurricanes based at Croydon had their revenge and only a few of the raiders managed to get back across the Channel.

Sunday, 18th August 1940 was a fine, sunny day with a little enemy activity, but at 1 o'clock a substantial flight of nearly 60 German aircraft crossed the southern coast. There also came a small group of nine Dornier 17s flying as low as 50 ft above the ground, avoiding radar. Their target – RAF Kenley. The Germans had intended that these nine aircraft should come in low over Kenley after the other aircraft had bombed the airfield from a higher altitude. In the event, the Dornier 17s got there first, flying over Bletchingley, then almost scraping the roofs of Caterham. One of them dropped a few small bombs over the town, hitting three cottages in Oak Road and killing a woman. Several other inhabitants were wounded and a horse pulling a milk float was also hit. The unfortunate animal was found dead between the shafts.

Over Kenley airfield the German aircraft did their worst – hangars were bombed with ease and various other buildings, including the hospital block, badly damaged or reduced to rubble. A little later bombs rained down from those aircraft flying in at altitude. However, the Germans came under heavy fire both from the ground and from defending Hurricanes. One Dornier was hit and crashed into a bun-

Mobile Nursing Unit No 2 at Caterham. These units attended the wounded after the enemy air-raid at Kenley in 1940.

164

501 Squadron at Kenley during the Battle of Britain in 1940. The aircraft in the background is a Hawker Hurricane.

galow. All the crew were killed but the five occupants of the building miraculously escaped from the burning ruins. A second Dornier was hit and crash-landed in a field near Biggin Hill, the crew surviving. At Kenley, ten British servicemen had not been so fortunate and were either killed or died later of their wounds.

Meanwhile, the attacking Hurricanes were also taking casualties as they chased the retreating German aircraft. During a dogfight over Worcester Park, a Hurricane was badly damaged but the pilot, realising that if he bailed out his aircraft might crash on the homes below, stayed with his machine. He attempted a landing in Morden Park but hit some trees and was killed. The author well remembers as a child being shown the spot where this brave young man gave his life for others. In 1971 Merton Technical College was built there, but the Hurricane pilot was not forgotten – on a wall of the building a commemorative plaque carries the inscription, '. . . erected by public subscription to honour the memory of No. 819018 Sergeant P.K. Walley, Battle of Britain pilot of 615 Squadron, Royal Auxiliary Air Force, 20 years old. Shot down by enemy raiders August 18th 1940. It is recalled with pride that, knowing he was about to crash, Sergeant Walley bravely managed to guide his badly damaged aircraft over nearby houses. Thereby safeguarding the lives of the residents.'

Sergeant Walley is remembered in Surrey today, just as are over 20,000 British and Commonwealth airmen who perished in the war but have no known grave. The impressive memorial to them stands on the hill overlooking the meadows of Runnymede, where over 700 years earlier the first step was taken towards the democracy which they died trying to preserve.

The German raid on Kenley was one small but significant incident in a long and painful war. On 4th September there was a terrible raid on the Vickers Aircraft Works near Brooklands which resulted in a large number of casualties. There were to be many more raids before the war was ended and, just as peace seemed within grasp, there came the fearful raids of the 'doodlebugs'. A large number of flying bombs dropped on Surre — five fell on Guildford and two on Godalming, twenty came down in the Dorking area killing a total of three residents. On 6th July 1944 one fell on County Hall at Kingston, but the council's staff carried on phlegmatically as usual. In August 1944 another came

Caterham Fire Brigade in 1942.

Brockham Civil Defence outside the church at Brockham Green in 1945.

straight down on Abinger parish church. Under the headline 'Bomb destroys Church' the local paper reported succinctly, 'A flying bomb fell on a country church in Southern England just before morning service was due to begin yesterday morning. As the bomb was falling the Rector was on his way to church. He was not injured. Rescue men, firemen and soldiers searched the rubble in case people had got to church early for the service, but no one was found.'

For all Surrey civilians the war meant the blackout, the fearful wailing of the air raid sirens, the hasty retreat to shelters on the playing fields, in the back garden or under the stairs, and rationing. Long after the war had ended the rationing continued and it was 1954 before the last of it was gone. The year before, in celebration of Coronation Day, most Surrey school children received a gift. For the author it was a cup and saucer, printed with a picture of the new queen, and the largest orange ever seen. The crockery was flung into the school bag to take its chance, the orange borne home like treasure from the East.

167

18

MODERN TIMES

The Coronation of our present Queen was the first to be watched on television by thousands of Surrey people. The event was a renewal of the camaraderie and sense of unity which had existed during the dark days of the war. Now, whole streets of people, sometimes crammed into one living room, sat glued to a nine inch square piece of glass. Outside there were street parties and parades in every town and village and optimism was in the air. The disappointing hardships following an expensive war had gone on far too long, but things were beginning to change. It was a time to rebuild – to throw out the old and bring in the new.

In Surrey, as in many other parts of Britain, 'bringing in the new' often meant the wholesale destruction of anything 'old' which was in the way. In many of our towns 'worthless' old buildings gave way to modern shops and tall office blocks and the human scale was lost. Other important factors also influenced the rapid changes taking place. As prosperity returned, the number of cars in the county began to increase dramatically. Planners sought to alter the town to fit the car. In Croydon, for example, during the 1960s the old town almost completely disappeared to be replaced with tower blocks and a town centre traffic fly-over. All this attracted the money of London city firms looking for cheaper office space and brought prosperity to the town. It is questionable whether it was a price well paid.

The Saxon town of Kingston also bowed to the pressures of developers but at least the character of its ancient market place has been retained. The Victorian railway towns of Woking and Redhill have also been extensively redeveloped in recent years. In Woking's case it seems to have happened twice in the last 15! Gone are most of the original buildings, just as the patina of age was beginning to make them collectable.

During the Second World War many scientific and military research units moved out of London into Surrey. As a result, in the late 1940s science-based companies developed as one of the mainstays of the county's industry. The aircraft manufacturers, Vickers at Weybridge

An idyllic rural scene at Compton in 1904 before the village became a shortcut for the motorist.

and Hawker at Kingston, formed the focal point for a wide range of engineering companies and component manufacturers. Commercial and public vehicle production continued on a large scale at the Dennis factory on the outskirts of Guildford. Throughout Surrey there was a large number of small-scale manufacturers making a plethora of different items, including electrical and plastic goods.

Between 1960 and 1980 the construction of modern office blocks in towns such as Guildford and Woking encouraged a number of large companies to base their administrative headquarters in the county. A survey undertaken in the 1970s as part of Surrey County Council's structure plan showed that about 60% of the working population of Woking were employed in the town. A further 15% commuted not to London but to other Surrey towns, whilst only 18% made the daily trip to the capital. This trend has continued into the 1990s and dispels the myth that Woking is a dormitory town in the heart of London's 'commuter belt'.

The early days of motoring are remembered each year with the London to Brighton Veteran Car Run which takes the cars through Surrey. (Surrey Mirror)

Since the war, most of Surrey's towns have been developed as commercial centres almost to the exclusion of all else. It is a rather bizarre fact that, as a result, the number of people living in the centres of our towns has dramatically fallen. Shops run by local people who lived above their businesses have given way to national chains who use the spare floors for office space or storage. Streets of terraced houses have been demolished to make way for car parks. Each town has sprouted suburbs of its own, where every home has on average more than one car. The car is now used to transport the suburb dweller back into the town where he once lived – the result is traffic chaos especially in the morning and evening!

In Guildford, the priority of the motor vehicle has given the town a gyratory road system, which has destroyed the character of the riverside areas and severed the ancient High Street from the Town Bridge over the river Wey. At the top of the county town's High Street, still paved with granite sets, a multi-storey car park towers over the Norman keep of Guildford castle, Holy Trinity church and much else besides. Only recently has such sacrifice been seen as folly. The result

170

A 'revivalist' coach crosses the river Ember in 1923 via 'The Splash' in Summer Road, East Molesey. The post-1968 flood prevention scheme has destroyed this view.

has been something of a reverse of policy, beginning with the increasing introduction of pedestrian-only shopping areas and 'park and ride' bus schemes. Plans to discourage drivers from bringing their vehicles into town are now seen as a priority.

Since the 1950s Surrey's varied and often beautiful countryside has been under constant threat. Major road schemes have been in progress somewhere in the county throughout the period and they continue. The ever-increasing traffic has brought about a plethora of road improvements, bypasses and, of course, the M25 motorway. A measure of the problem for planners can be appreciated after ten seconds of standing, for example, in Esher High Street. When the town was bypassed many thought a rural peace would descend upon the place but now, after only a few years, the traffic is as heavy as before.

The flood of suburban building has been contained, to a great extent, by the green belt policy, which aims to retain a circle of countryside

The Peacocks shopping and entertainments centre in Woking was opened in April 1992. As well as popular shops, the centre includes cinemas, two theatres, a restaurant and café plus the town's public library. (Michael Hutt)

The pattern of roof beams of the White Lion Walk shopping precinct in Guildford, opened in 1986. The lion once graced the frontage of the White Lion Inn, later the Lion Hotel, which occupied the site between North Street and the High Street until 1956. (Michael Hutt)

around London. But there have been many pressures on the green belt and recent comments from central government, hinting at a relaxation of these policies. Meanwhile a great deal of 'infilling' has taken place, the results of which can be seen in pleasant estates adjacent to several Surrey towns.

Even the skies over Surrey have become overcrowded. Although only a baggage terminal at Heathrow is officially in Surrey, and Gatwick was transferred to West Sussex in 1974, a huge number of aircraft overfly the county. Noise is a constant problem for those living under the flight-paths.

With all these threats it seems amazing that the unique nature of the Surrey countryside still survives – or is it just an illusion? Is there anything left to save? The answer has to be an emphatic 'yes'. Salmon now swim again in the river Thames for the first time in 160 years. Parts of south-west Surrey are home to several rare species of bird and animal found in very few other places in Britain. Many areas of rural Britain have become featureless prairies of winter wheat, with hedges removed and trees chopped down. In contrast, within the gardens of suburban Surrey, birds and butterflies, foxes and frogs have found a safe sanctuary.

More than ever there are groups of Surrey people dedicated to the restoration and preservation of both the natural environment and those man-made features which are an integral part of our county's history. This enthusiasm to discover and record as much as possible about the county's past is reflected in the huge number of active local history and archaeology groups and societies that exist in almost every town and village. The Surrey Archaeological Society was founded in 1854 and it continues to be a focal point for research at all levels. But from Nutfield to Newdigate, Wonersh to Walton-on-the-Hill, groups of enthusiasts are rediscovering the rich legacy that is Surrey's past.

Many people have been hard at work restoring those important physical features of the landscape such as village ponds, antique gardens and waterways. At Normandy, for example, a local group has spent thousands of hours bringing their pond back to its former glory. At Painshill near Cobham, the impossible has been achieved and a unique 18th century garden has been saved from dereliction. But the prize for dedication and persistence must go to those who have brought the Basingstoke Canal back to life again.

From almost any high vantage point in the Surrey hills such as Box Hill, Leith Hill, Anstiebury or Hydon's Ball, the southern view is of a seemingly endless green countryside stretching to the horizon of the Sussex Downs. But it is a man-made landscape, where the conflicts between land use and preservation will never go away. It is up to all of us to ensure that the balance is kept and a landscape maintained which will always be uniquely Surrey.

Appendix 1

THE PRINCIPAL TOWNS OF SURREY

Banstead

Banstead is first recorded in a grant of Caedwalla, King of Wessex, in AD 680. By Domesday it was held by the Bishop of Bayeux, Richard of Odo. The church dates from the late 12th and early 13th century. There was horse racing on Banstead Downs as early as 1625 and a race was used as an excuse for the gathering of the Earl of Holland's Royalist forces on the Downs in 1648. Banstead station was opened in 1865. A lunatic asylum, later known as the London County Lunatic Asylum opened here in 1877.

Bletchingley

Bletchingley is first recorded in Domesday in 1086, but the name probably has 7th or early 8th century origins. It means 'the clearing or ley of the people of Blaecci'. A castle was built here soon after the Norman Conquest as the Surrey base of the de Clare family. It was dismantled in about 1264 during the fight between Simon de Montfort and Henry III. Blechingley was a borough by 1225 but, like Reigate, it was a borough created by the Lord of the Manor with the king's permission rather than by royal charter. An annual fair was granted in 1283, by which time the place was a thriving market town and centre for the fulling and weaving of woollen cloth. Thereafter Blechingley declined and only 70 households were recorded in the Hearth Tax Returns of 1664. It continued to be represented in Parliament until the Reform Act of 1832 but is now little more than a large but attractive village. Incidentally, the modern spelling of the village as 'Bletchingley' is strongly opposed by most of its inhabitants!

Camberley

Camberley is a Victorian development which owes its origins to the opening of the Staff College in 1862. At first the settlement near the college was called Cambridge Town after the then commander-in-chief of the army, the Duke of Cambridge. Because of confusion with the university town and resulting mis-direction of post, the name was changed to Camberley. Camberley railway station opened in 1878.

Caterham
The first reference to Caterham was in the 12th century but it was always an insignificant village until the arrival of the railway in 1856. The opening of the Guards' Depot in 1877 gave the settlement an important boost.

Chertsey
Chertsey Abbey was founded in about AD 666 and this settlement has the distinction of being the earliest to be mentioned in a document when the abbey was endowed in AD 673. It is difficult to say exactly when the homes and businesses of a lay community were first built adjacent to the abbey. A market and fair were granted to Chertsey by Henry I in 1135 and the town gained a second fair by a charter of 1440. The abbey was dissolved in 1537 but this seems to have had little effect upon the prosperity of the town. In the Hearth Tax Returns of 1664 it was assessed as the fourth largest town in Surrey with 167 households. Its riverside location made it particularly popular during the 18th century. Chertsey is situated at a crossing of the Thames and the first bridge here dates from the early 15th century but the present bridge was built in the 1780s. The railway came to the town in 1848. Chertsey became part of the Runnymede District in 1974.

Croydon
From the 12th century, at least, Croydon was a favoured summer residence for the Archbishops of Canterbury, although their ownership of the manor goes back before AD 871. The palace was sold in 1780 and then used for a variety of industrial uses, including fabric printing and bleaching. Fortunately, much of its medieval fabric has survived and towards the end of the last century it became a school. Archbishop Kilwardby received a grant to hold a weekly market and an annual fair at Croydon from Edward I in 1276. A further market and fair were granted in 1314 and yet another market and fair in 1343. The town was not, however, incorporated as an independent borough until 1883. The world's first public railway, the horse-drawn Surrey Iron Railway, opened from Wandsworth to Croydon in 1803. Six years later the town was connected to the Thames by the Croydon Canal but that was a short-lived affair. Much of its channel was filled in and used for the

trackbed of the first steam railway to reach Croydon in 1839. Croydon became a county borough in 1888 and the centre of a London Borough of the same name in 1965.

Dorking

The place name, 'Deorc Ingas', has 7th or 8th century origins and means 'the people of Deorc'. However, evidence has been found in the town in recent years to suggest that here there was a Roman settlement on Stane Street, the Roman road from London to Chichester. Dorking is first mentioned in Domesday in 1086 and there was certainly a market here by 1278. It was an important market by the 14th century and continued in the High Street until 1926. The administration of Dorking has a complicated history. At one time the town was divided into three tithings called boroughs, which together had 185 households in the Hearth Tax Returns of 1664. The railway came to the town in 1849. The importance of Dorking as an agricultural centre is emphasized by its own breed of five-clawed Dorking chicken, which has become the emblem of the town.

Egham

The manor of Egham was held by Chertsey Abbey until the Dissolution in 1537. Magna Carta was sealed at Runnymede near here in 1215. The Regency parish church is something of a rarity in Surrey but was described by Ian Nairn as 'very ugly'. Egham station opened in 1856. Royal Holloway College for Women opened here in 1886. Designed by W.H. Crossland and paid for by Thomas Holloway who made his fortune from his famous pills and ointment, it is undoubtedly one of the most impressive Victorian buildings in Britain. Holloway also financed the nearby sanatorium.

Epsom

The earliest reference to Epsom is in AD 727 in relation to a grant of land to Chertsey Abbey. The manor was the property of the abbey in 1086 and remained so until the Dissolution in 1537. Over the centuries the name changed from Evesham to various forms of Ebbisham through to Ebsame and finally Epsom. As a small village it was unimportant until the discovery of the Epsom wells on the nearby common in the 17th century. Horse racing on the Downs also became popular at the time. The 'Oaks' was first run at Epsom in 1779 and the 'Derby' the following year. Later Epsom developed a thriving market. The first railway station opened here in 1847. In the late 19th century the area around Epsom became home for a number of mental institutions and asylums.

Esher

The manor of Esher was given by William the Conqueror to the abbot and convent of Croix St Leufroy in Normandy. Later it passed to the Bishop of Winchester. A priory was founded nearby at Sandon (now Sandown) in the 12th century but all the monks were wiped out by the plague in 1349. Sandown Park racecourse was opened here in 1875 and the small pond, which gives its name to the famous 'Pond Fence', is said by some to be the remnant of the priory fishpond. Esher station opened in 1838 with the uninspiring name of 'Ditton Marsh', but this did not stop Esher developing into a very fashionable residential area, particularly because of the proximity of Claremont with its royal connections.

Farnham

The name means 'enclosure in the bracken' and the earliest surviving reference to Farnham is in a charter dated to about AD 688. Domesday records the ownership of the Bishop of Winchester, Henry de Blois, who probably built the first castle here shortly after 1066. The castle continued to be an important residence for successive bishops right up until 1927. Farnham was a borough by the grant of the bishop by 1207 and was given a market and fair in 1216. By the end of the 17th century the market had developed into one of the largest corn markets in the country. The town suffered a short decline during the Civil War, especially due to the billeting of troops in relation to the various episodes which took place at the castle. By 1664 Farnham had recovered and in the Hearth Tax Returns it was the second largest town in Surrey with 293 households. Farnham's wealth during the Georgian and Victorian period was based on hop growing and there were still many acres of hopfields around the town until well into this century. The modern growth of the town dates from the arrival of the railway in 1852.

Godalming

The name of Godalming (Godhelm's Ingas) means literally 'the people of Godhelm' and this Saxon clan probably settled here in the 7th or early 8th century. The manor of Godalming was first mentioned in the will of Alfred the Great in about AD 880. By 1086 it was a substantial property with three mills and two churches. It was architectural writer Ian Nairn who in 1962 succinctly described the main reason for the town's later growth, 'Godalming is a rarity among English country towns in that it has no central open space of any sort ... Perhaps the explanation is that Guildford is only four miles away and that Godalming had been an industrial town ... rather than a rural centre.' These industries were clothmaking, hosiery manufacture, tanning and skin-working, papermaking and stone-quarrying. The town also gained prosperity from its position on the Portsmouth road. Godalming was granted a market and fair by Edward I in 1300 and created a borough by Elizabeth I in 1575. The Hearth Tax Returns of 1664 list 166 households within the borough, making it the fifth largest town in the county with only one household less than Chertsey. The railway reached Godalming from Guildford in 1849, the line being extended to Havant and thus to Portsmouth in 1859. Godalming was the first town in the world to have a public electricity supply service. It remained an independent borough until it was absorbed into the new Waverley District in 1974.

Guildford

The name of the town probably means the 'Golden Ford', from the yellow sand of the bed of the river Wey at this ancient crossing point. Like Godalming, Guildford is mentioned in the will of Alfred the Great in about AD 880. By the late Saxon period it had developed into an important commercial centre with a mint, replacing Eashing as the 'burh' of the area. The layout of the town's major streets is clearly the product of Saxon town planning. The strategic value of the town, guarding an important focus of communications, was quickly recognised by the Normans, who began building the castle soon after 1066. The castle became an important royal residence during the 12th and 13th centuries but thereafter fell into decay. In the Surrey Domesday, apart from Southwark which is no longer in the county, Guildford is the only settlement given town status. The town may have become a borough during the 10th century, although the earliest documentary evidence dates to 1130. Guildford later developed as an important clothmaking town and its famous inns and taverns prospered from travellers on the Portsmouth road. The Hearth Tax Returns of 1664 list 371 households in the town. The railway came to Guildford in 1845 as a branch from Woking. In 1927 the town became the centre of the new Diocese of Guildford and in 1961 the cathedral on Stag Hill was consecrated by the Queen. Guildford is the county town of Surrey, whatever arguments there may be to the contrary, for it is at Guildford that the High Sheriff of Surrey proclaims the new monarch, as last happened in 1952. Above all Guildford is the main marketing centre for a wide area of west Surrey.

Haslemere

The name literally means 'the place with hazel trees by a pool'. It is said that at least part of the pool survived until 1859. Haslemere is not mentioned in Domesday, when it was presumably part of the manor

179

of Godalming, the oldest surviving reference to it dating from about 1180. By 1221 the manor of Godalming was the property of the Bishop of Salisbury and he was granted a market for Haslemere in that year, which may also mark the date when Haslemere was established on its present site. There is some evidence to suggest that prior to that date the settlement was either centred around the parish church or on Haste Hill overlooking the present town. Haslemere was granted a fair in 1394, whilst the same charter also confirmed the market. The woollen industry and ironworking seem have been important factors in the town's economy. Haslemere declined during the Tudor period until a charter from Elizabeth I in 1596 restored the market and fair and confirmed the right of the town to send two members to Parliament. The Hearth Tax Returns record only 82 households in Haslemere in 1664. The size of the electorate was therefore always small and it remained firmly a 'pocket borough' until losing its MPs in the reforms of 1832. Haslemere's most famous MP was James Oglethorpe, founder of the State of Georgia. The railway came to Haslemere in 1859 and rescued the town from obscurity. Thereafter it developed as a popular residential area in the 'heart of the country', particularly for artists and writers. Tennyson's house, Aldworth, is very near the town, although it is actually just over the border in Sussex.

Horley
Horley is not mentioned in Domesday and the earliest surviving references date from the 13th century, when the manor was the property of Chertsey Abbey. It remained abbey land until the Dissolution in 1537. The character of Horley began to change from small Wealden village to small town, when the London to Brighton railway was constructed through the parish and a station opened in 1841. With the post-Second World War expansion of the adjacent Gatwick aerodrome into an international airport, the town of Horley has grown rapidly.

Kingston upon Thames
Kingston was important as a royal residence perhaps as early as the 7th century, hence the name. Later no less than seven Saxon kings were crowned here, including Edward the Martyr. The coronation stone upon which it is alleged the kings sat during the ceremony is preserved beside the Guildhall. Kingston developed as a market town and important centre for river traffic at a ford on the river Thames. By 1219 the first bridge had been built and it was often to prove of strategic value during rebellion and civil war, being the first bridge upstream of London. The railway bypassed Kingston in 1838 and spawned the suburb of Surbiton.

It finally arrived in the town in 1868. Kingston expanded rapidly as a result and became an important retailing centre, with department stores such as the famous Bentalls. By the 1920s the town was already sinking beneath the tide of building, its streets jammed with motor cars. As a result, in 1926 it was bypassed again – this time by a road – the first bypass to be built in Britain.

Leatherhead

Like several other places in Surrey, the earliest surviving reference to Leatherhead occurs in the will of Alfred the Great in about AD 880. The Domesday entry for Leatherhead includes the church, which still has some possible late Saxon features. Situated almost at the centre of the county, Leatherhead can claim to have once been the county town – certainly the county court is thought to have been held here until its removal to Guildford. The town was granted a market and fair by Henry III in 1248 but was almost totally destroyed by fire in 1392. Although the town was rebuilt, decline set in and its market ceased sometime during the Tudor period. The Hearth Tax Returns of 1664 record 122 households in the town. The railway reached Leatherhead in 1859.

Merton

The earliest surviving record of the manor of Merton is in a grant of King Edgar in AD 967 and at the time of Domesday it was a royal manor. Merton Priory was founded here on the banks of the river Wandle in 1114. Nelson and Lady Hamilton lived at Merton after England's most famous admiral had purchased Merton Place in 1801. Merton's numerous mills have been utilised by many industries over the centuries, including papermaking and calico printing. In 1861 William Morris founded a firm to design and produce fabrics, glass and furniture which had its works at Merton. The first railway station here was opened in 1868.

Mitcham

At the time of Domesday, Mitcham was the property of the Bishop of Bayeux, but the earliest reference to the manor may date from the 8th century. Sir Walter Raleigh had a house here. The soil of the area was ideal for 'physic' gardens where peppermint, lavender, roses, camomile and liquorice were amongst the variety of plants grown. The river Wandle flows through Mitcham, where there were a number of mills for various industrial activities such as calico bleaching and snuff manufacture. In the last century it was famous for its 'Mitcham Mints' and 'Mitcham Shag Tobacco'.

Redhill

The small settlement of Redhill developed into a substantial town during the 1860s. The catalyst was its position at a railway junction. The line from London to Brighton opened through Redhill in 1841 and a year later came the line to Tonbridge. In 1849 the line to Guildford via Reigate and Dorking was completed. In recent years many of Redhill's Victorian buildings have been demolished and the town redeveloped with modern shopping precincts.

Reigate

The original settlement of Reigate was clustered around the parish church, some distance to the east of the present town, and is listed in Domesday under its original name of Cherchefelle. Reigate Castle was probably originally constructed soon after the Conquest and later became the main Surrey residence of the de Warrennes, sometime Earls of Surrey. Around the castle the new town of Reigate grew up – the earliest record of the name dating from about 1170. Reigate had a market by 1276 and was identified as a borough in 1291, although not by royal charter. The Hearth Tax Returns of 1664 list 154 households in the town. Reigate's later administrative history is complicated but it was finally constituted as a borough by royal charter in 1863. The railway reached the town in 1849. In 1974 Reigate became part of the Reigate and Banstead District.

Richmond

Richmond was originally known as Sheen. It was not recorded in Domesday, presumably as it was part of Kingston. However, by the 12th century Sheen had become a separate manor. It became a popular royal residence especially during the reign of Edward III, who probably built the first palace here. He died at Sheen in 1377. The palace was demolished by Richard II and rebuilt by Henry V. Henry VII reconstructed it and called it Richmond, after the earldom he had held – hence the change of name. Elizabeth I died here in 1603. Now only the gatehouse of the palace survives. Richmond became a popular riverside resort during the Georgian period. The railway came to the town in 1846 and Richmond became a Greater London Borough in 1965.

Staines

A settlement at Staines was established by the Romans and called 'Pontibus', meaning 'at the bridges' – one bridge carried the important road from London to Silchester over the Thames and the other crossed a branch of the river Colne. The first known reference to the present name, meaning 'stones', was in AD 969. At the time of Domesday, Staines belonged to Westminster Abbey but passed to the Crown after the Dissolution and then in 1613 to Lord Knyvett of Stanwell. The weekly market was granted in 1228. The present bridge over the Thames, designed by George Rennie, was opened in 1832. The railway arrived in 1848. Here there was an important linoleum works and also Ashby's famous brewery. Staines was part of Middlesex until 1965.

Sutton

In 1086 Sutton was the property of Chertsey Abbey. Following the dissolution of the abbey in 1537, Sutton passed to Henry VIII and then to Sir Nicholas Carew. During the turnpike days, the inns of Sutton, especially The Cock, flourished as they catered for travellers on the Brighton road. The railway came to Sutton in 1847 and by the end of the century a typical suburban town had developed. Sutton became the centre of a London Borough in 1965.

Walton-on-Thames

At the time of Domesday, Walton was held by Edward of Salisbury. Henry VIII granted Walton two fairs in 1516 – one at Easter and the other in October. On St George's Hill to the south-west is an Iron Age hillfort now partly built on. It was here in 1649 that an interesting early experiment in Socialism took place. A group calling themselves 'Diggers', who combined social and religious ideals and were led by Gerrard Winstanley, began to till the waste, planting root crops and beans. The first bridge at Walton was built in 1750 and the railway arrived here in 1838. In this century Walton became famous for its film studios. It has been part of Elmbridge District since 1974.

Weybridge

At the time of Domesday, land at Weybridge was held by Chertsey Abbey, the Bishop of Bayeux and an unnamed Englishman. By 1239 the entire manor was in the hands of Geoffrey de Lucy. Later, Weybridge became a royal manor and at Oatlands nearby Henry VIII began building a palace in 1538. It was demolished about 1650. The date of Weybridge's first bridge is unknown but there must have been one here over the Wey by the time of the Norman Conquest. Weybridge station, situated in a deep cutting, was opened in 1838.

Woking

The original Saxon settlement of Woking (Old Woking) is on the banks of the river Wey to the south-east of the present town. The name means 'people of Wocc' and, like Dorking and Godalming, refers to the clan of an individual Saxon, who settled here. Near Old Woking there was once an important royal palace which was used by both Henry VII and Henry VIII. It was here that the 'Treaty of Woking' between Henry VII and Maximilian of Austria was signed in 1497. The present town, adjacent to the railway built here in 1838, has its origins in the purchase of most of Woking Common for use as a cemetery by the London Necropolis and National Mausoleum Company in 1852. Three years later there began a series of sales of substantial sections of the land for development. Thus the new town of Woking was born which now, in terms of population, is the largest town in Surrey.

Appendix 2

A SURREY CHRONOLOGY

54 BC	Julius Caesar and his army marched through the area on their way to attack the Catuvellauni.
AD 43	Roman invasion of Britain.
410	The supposed date by which all the Roman legions had been withdrawn from Britain.
420	About this date the first Saxons arrived as mercenaries.
500	Battle of Mons Bardonicus.
568	Battle of Wibbandun.
596	St Augustine was sent by Pope Gregory to convert the pagan Saxons to Christianity.
650	About this time London was re-established as a major port and commercial centre.
666	Chertsey Abbey founded.
673	First surviving documentary record of Sudergeona' or Surrey.
789	The first Vikings landed in Britain.
823	King Egbert of Wessex defeated the Mercians and men of Kent thus bringing most of southern England, including Surrey, under the rule of Wessex.
851	Saxon victory over the Danes at the battle of Ockley.
871	Alfred the Great became King of Wessex.
890	About this time the 'burh' at Eashing was constructed.
893	Danish army defeated at Farnham.
899	King Alfred died.
902–958	During this time six Saxon kings were crowned at Kingston.
1017	Cnut became King of England.
1036	Alfred, son of King Ethelred, was murdered and his followers massacred at Guildford.
1066	Norman conquest of England.
1070	Guildford Castle first constructed at about this date.

1086	Domesday Book.
1114	Priory founded at Merton.
1128	Waverley Abbey founded.
1215	King John put his seal to Magna Carta at Runnymede.
1235	Reigate Priory founded.
1264	Rebellion of Simon de Montfort.
1348/49	The Black Death.
1381	Peasants' Revolt.
1497	Cornish rebels involved in skirmish at Guildford.
1536	Reigate and Tandridge Priories, Waverley Abbey dissolved.
1537	Chertsey Abbey dissolved.
1538	The building of Nonsuch Palace commenced.
1554	Rebellion against Queen Mary led by Thomas Wyatt. The rebels crossed Kingston Bridge on their way to London.
1558	Elizabeth became Queen.
1588	Defeat of the Spanish Armada by English fleet led by Lord Howard of Effingham.
1603	Elizabeth I died at Richmond Palace.
1611	George Abbot became Archbishop of Canterbury.
1620	John Evelyn born at Wotton.
1625	Charles I became King.
1633	George Abbot died.
1636	Charles I created Richmond Park.
1642	First battles of Civil War. Royalists seized Farnham Castle but Parliamentary troops led by Waller regained it.
1643	'Battle of Farnham Park'.
1648	'Battle of Surbiton Common'.
1653	Wey Navigation opened.
1663	Samuel Pepys drank at the Epsom wells.
1685	Nonsuch Palace demolished about this date.
1698	Tsar Peter the Great of Russia stayed at Godalming.
1732	James Oglethorpe sailed from England to found the State of Georgia.
1764	Godalming Navigation opened.
1780	The first Derby run at Epsom.
1794	Basingstoke Canal opened.
1803	Surrey Iron Railway opened – the world's first public railway, albeit horse-drawn.
1832	Reform Act – 'rotten boroughs' like Gatton lost their MPs.

1837	Queen Victoria ascended the throne.
1838	First steam railway in Surrey opened to Woking.
1852	London Necropolis established at Woking.
1853	Queen Victoria reviewed her troops on Chobham Common.
1875	Sandown Park Racecourse opened.
1881	World's first public electricity supply service founded at Godalming.
1889	First Surrey County Council created.
1901	Queen Victoria died.
1907	Brooklands motor track opened. A. Verdon-Roe made first aeroplane flight in Britain at Brooklands.
1915	Zeppelin raid over Guildford.
1926	Britain's first bypass opened at Kingston.
1940	German air raid on Kenley Aerodrome on 18th August. Many casualties after German bombing raid on Vickers aircraft factory at Brooklands on 4th September.
1944	Doodlebug destroyed Abinger church.
1953	Countywide celebrations for Elizabeth II's Coronation.
1965	Greater London Council created.
1968	Serious floods in September. Surrey University opened.
1972	Work began on the M25.
1974	Local government reorganisation created new district councils. Gatwick Airport became part of West Sussex.
1985	M25 completed.

BIBLIOGRAPHY

Here is a complete list of the books and articles which I have consulted during the writing of this history.

Alexander, Matthew *Guildford: A Short History* Ammonite Books, 1992

Aston, Shirley B. *A History of West Horsley* H.W. Forder, 1974

Aubrey, John *The Natural History and Antiquities of the County of Surrey*, 5 vols 1718/19

Bird, Joanna & D.G. (Editors) *The Archaeology of Surrey to 1540* Surrey Archaeological Society, 1987

Black, J.B. *The Reign of Elizabeth 1558–1603* 2nd edition OUP, 1959

Blackman, M.E. & Pulford, J.S.L. *A Short History of Weybridge* Walton & Weybridge Local History Society, 1991

Brakspear, Harold *Waverley Abbey* Surrey Archaeological Society, 1905

Brandon, Peter *A History of Surrey* Phillimore, 1977

Brayley, E.W. *History of Surrey* 5 vols, 1841

Burns, David *The Sheriffs of Surrey* Phillimore, 1992

Carter, Ernest F. *The Story of Redhill as a Railway Centre* Holmesdale. 1955

Clark, R.H. *A Southern Region Record* The Oakwood Press, 1964

Clarke, John M. *The Brookwood Necropolis Railway* 2nd edition The Oakwood Press, 1988

Cook, Alan *Oatlands Palace Excavations 1968: Interim Report* Surrey Archaeological Collections, Vol 71, 1969

Cooper, P.M. *The Story of Claremont* 4th edition West Brothers, 1968

Corke, Shirley *Guildford: A Pictorial Record* Phillimore, 1990

Crocker, Glenys *Chilworth Gunpowder* Surrey Industrial History Group, 1984

Crocker, Glenys (Editor) *A Guide to the Industrial Archaeology of Surrey* Association for Industrial Archaeology, 1990

Darby, H.C. & Campbell, E.M.J. (Editors) *The Domesday Geography of South-East England* Cambridge University Press, 1962

Dedman, Stanley *Some Personalities of Godalming's History* Godalming Branch Library, 1969

Dent, John *The Quest for Nonsuch* Hutchinson, 1962

Drewett, Peter & Others *The South East to AD 1000* Longman, 1988

Dunlop, Ian *Palaces and Progresses of Elizabeth I* Cape, 1962

East, Katherine & others *A Viking Sword Found at Chertsey* Surrey Archaeological Collections, Vol 76, 1984

Epsom Wells: a New History of Epsom Wells and Epsom Salts Epsom & Ewell Borough Council, 1989

Evelyn, John *The Diary of John Evelyn* Selected and edited by John Bowle OUP, 1985

Festing, Sally *The Story of Lavender* 2nd edition Heritage in Sutton Leisure, 1989

Fiennes, Celia *The Journeys of Celia Fiennes* Edited by Christopher Morris The Cresset Press, 1947

Flint, Peter *R.A.F. Kenley* Terence Dalton Ltd, 1985

Grimwood-Taylor, James L. '. . . Sind Destroyers of Mashines' Article in *Stamp News*, 20th June 1984

Hall, Derek & Angela *Farnham and the Civil War: a Historical Review* Farnham Museum Society, 1973

Harding, Joan & Banks, Joyce *Newdigate: its History and Houses,* 1993

Harrison, Frederic *Annals of an Old Manor-House: Sutton Place, Guildford* Abridged edition Macmillan, 1899

Heales, Alfred *The History of Tanridge Priory, Surrey* 1885

Hearnshaw, F.J.C. *The Place of Surrey in the History of England* Macmillan, 1936

Home, Gordon *A Guide to Epsom* The Homeland Association, 1902

Hughes, G.M. *A History of Windsor Forest, Sunninghill and the Great Park* Ballantyne, Hanson and Co, 1890

Jackson, Alan A. (Editor) *Dorking: A Surrey Market Town through Twenty Centuries* Dorking Local History Group, 1991

Janaway, John *Godalming: A Short History* Ammonite Books, 1993

Janaway, John 'Martin Tupper, the forgotten poet and author of Surrey' Article in the *Surrey Advertiser*, 1st December 1989

Janaway, John *Surrey: A Photographic Record 1850–1920* Countryside Books, 1984

Kenyon, G.H. *The Glass Industry of the Weald* Leicester University Press, 1967

Ketteringham, Lesley L. *Alsted. Excavation of a Thirteenth-Fourteenth Century Sub-Manor House* Surrey Archaeological Research Volume No. 2, 1976

Knight, David *Dorking in Wartime,* The Author, 1989

Lister, Lalage *Nonsuch: Pearl of the Realm* Sutton Leisure Services, 1992

Lasham, Frank *Palaeolithic Man in West Surrey* Surrey Archaeological Collections, Vol 11, 1893

Lord, Maurice E. *Egham Races 1734–1884* Egham-by-Runnymede Historical Society, 1988

Malden, H.E. *A History of Surrey* Elliot Stock, 1900

Malden, H.E. *The Victoria History of the County of Surrey* 4 vols Constable, 1902

Morris, John (Editor) *Domesday Book: Surrey* Phillimore, 1975

Morris, Joseph E *Haslemere & Hindhead* The Homeland Association, 1910

Nairn, Ian & Pevsner, Nikolaus *The Buildings of England: Surrey* 2nd edition Penguin, 1971

Newbery, Celia (Editor) *A History of Sports in Dorking* The Local History Group of Dorking and Leith Hill Preservation Society, 1985

Noyes, Ann E. *Poverty and the Poor Law in Shere and Gomshall, 1780–1840* Portsmouth Polytechnic dissertation, 1991

O'Connell, Martin *Historic Towns in Surrey* Surrey Archaeological Society Research Volume No. 5, 1977

Pepys, Samuel *The Diary of Samuel Pepys* G. Bell, 1949

Poole, A.L. *From Domesday to Magna Carta, 1087–1216* 2nd edition OUP, 1955

Poulton, Rob *The Archaeological Investigations on the Site of Chertsey Abbey* Surrey Archaeological Research Volume No. 11, 1988

Poulton, Rob *Guildford Castle and Royal Palace* Surrey County Council, 1993

Poulton, Rob *Saxon Secrets in Surrey* Esso, 1990

Poulton, Rob & Woods, Humphrey *Excavations on the Site of the Dominican Friary at Guildford in 1974 and 1978* Surrey Archaeological Society Research Volume No. 9, 1984

Renn, Derek F. *The River Wey Bridges between Farnham and Guildford* Research Volume of Surrey Archaeological Society No. 1, pp 75–83, 1974

Robbins, Michael *Middlesex* Collins, 1953

Robinson, David *Pastors, Parishes and People in Surrey* Phillimore, 1989

Robinson, David *Surrey Through the Century 1889–1989* Surrey County Council, 1989

Salter, Brian J. (Editor) *Epsom Town, Downs and Common* Living History Publications, 1976

Scears, Ernest *A History of Reigate Priory* c1950

Sowan, Paul W. *Firestone and Hearthstone Mines in the Upper Greensand of East Surrey* Reprinted from the Proceedings of the Geologists' Association, Vol 86, Part 4, 1975

Stenton, Sir Frank *Anglo-Saxon England* 3rd edition OUP, 1971

Stevenson, William *General View of the Agriculture of the County of Surrey* Richard Phillips, 1809

Stonebanks, J. *Coway Stakes at Walton-on-Thames* Walton & Weybridge Local History Society, 1972

Swete, C.J. *A Handbook of Epsom 1860* Reprinted by EP Publishing, 1973.

Tooke, Jean *Bygone Caterham* Phillimore, 1988

Townsend, J.L. *The History of the Dorking Greystone Lime Co. Ltd and the Locomotive 'Townsend Hook'* Narrow Gauge Railway Society, 1961

Tupper, Martin F. *Stephan Langton: or the Days of King John* 1858

Vine, P.A.L. *Surrey Waterways* Middleton Press, 1987

Wakeford, Iain *Woking 150: the History of Woking and its Railway* The Mayford & Woking District History Society, 1987

Ware, Gwen *The White Monks of Waverley* Farnham & District Museum Society, 1976

Wheeler, Lucy *Chertsey Abbey: An Existence from the Past* Wells Gardner, Darton & Co., 1905

Whitbourn, John 'Day Guildford was Invaded by 15,000 Cornish Rebels' Article in the *Surrey Advertiser*, 2nd June 1989

Whitelock, Dorothy (Editor) *The Anglo-Saxon Chronicle: A Revised Translation* Eyre and Spottiswoode, 1961

Winter, Tim & Collyer, Graham *Around Haslemere and Hindhead in Old Photographs* Alan Sutton, 1991

Wood, Eric S. *A 16th Century Glasshouse at Knightons, Alfold, Surrey* Surrey Archaeological Collections, Vol 73, pp 1–47, 1982

Index